St. Paul's Eight Steps to Happiness

Other books by Kevin Vost
from Sophia Institute Press:

Memorize the Faith!

Fit for Eternal Life!

You Are That Temple!

The One-Minute Aquinas

Unearthing Your Ten Talents

Aquinas on the Four Last Things

12 Life Lessons from St. Thomas Aquinas

The Seven Gifts of the Holy Spirit

The Catholic Guide to Loneliness

How to Think Like Aquinas

The Seven Deadly Sins

Hounds of the Lord

Kevin Vost, Psy.D.

St. Paul's Eight Steps to Happiness

SOPHIA INSTITUTE PRESS
Manchester, New Hampshire

Cover by LUCAS Art & Design, Jenison, MI.

On the cover: *Saint Paul* (1482) by Bartolomeo Montagna,
Wikimedia Commons, public domain.

Sophia Institute Press
Box 5284, Manchester, NH 03108
1-800-888-9344
www.SophiaInstitute.com

paperback ISBN 978-1-64413-776-5

ebook ISBN 978-1-64413-777-2

Library of Congress Control Number: 2023942098

First printing

In Memoriam

This is Kevin Vost's final work, published posthumously. Kevin was unmatched in his ability to communicate Catholic truths in a clear and compelling way. Sophia Institute Press is honored to have worked closely with him for two decades, and we pray for the repose of his soul and peace and healing for his family.

Contents

St. Paul's Eight Steps to Happiness

Introduction

The Wisdom of St. Paul—Not Just for Philippians

O the depth of the riches and wisdom and knowledge of God!
How unsearchable are his judgments and how inscrutable his ways!

—Romans 11:33

For God is my witness, how I yearn for you all with the affection of Christ Jesus. And it is my prayer that your love may abound more and more, with knowledge and all discernment, so that you may approve what is excellent, and may be pure and blameless for the day of Christ, filled with the fruits of righteousness which come through Jesus Christ, to the glory and praise of God.

—Philippians 1:8–11

How This Book Came About

St. Paul knew well how God's ways and plans far exceed our understanding—and sometimes leave us gaping in surprise at what He has in store for us! Such was certainly the case for one Christian-persecuting Saul of Tarsus, later far better known as St. Paul, and honored with the title "the Apostle" by no less than St. Thomas Aquinas, the Church's Angelic Doctor.

I can identify with Paul's story to a certain extent. I spent twenty-five years of my early adulthood as an atheist, and though I did not persecute Christians, I certainly did nothing to bring anyone to Christ. That is, until I got knocked off my high horse (so to speak) and the scales fell from my eyes, when the Holy Spirit led me to the wisdom of St. Thomas Aquinas, and my faith was restored with my reason left intact.

As I look back to the days of yore before I left the Church, I recall that the Confirmation name I chose as a child happened to be Paul. I think it was because I liked the sound of the name and had a friend named Paul. As a childhood fan of Superman, and a burgeoning young weightlifter, had I known that *paulus* in Latin meant "little or small," I am pretty sure I would not have chosen that name!

I appreciate God's humor now, half a century later, when I reflect on what an appropriate choice it was. Even in my years of atheism, I greatly appreciated the Greco-Roman heritage of Western civilization in philosophy, politics, and law and in how it inspired the formation and Constitution of the United States of America. When I returned to Christ and His Church in my early forties, I came to understand the transcendent truth, beauty, and goodness of our Judeo-Christian heritage as well, with no loss of respect for what came from the best of the classical Greeks and Romans. Well, in Paul we have a Jew, a Roman citizen who knew Greek philosophy and wrote his scriptural letters in Greek and who became the greatest evangelist of Christ to the Gentiles. Paul, then, is the supreme embodiment of a Judeo-Christian, Greco-Roman four-in-one-special! Recently, I was happy to find that one very prominent Christian, indeed—our late pope emeritus, Benedict XVI—had highlighted this about Paul as well.[1]

Moving beyond my ancient personal history and getting down to how this book came about: it started forming in my mind when, in 2016, I was invited to give a talk at the Thomas Aquinas Forum hosted by the Office of Catechetics at Aquinas College, run by the wonderful Dominican Sisters of St. Cecilia

[1] For example: "Some have defined Paul as 'a man of three cultures,' taking into account his Jewish background, his Greek tongue and his prerogative as a '*civis romanus*' [Roman citizen], as the name of Latin origin suggests." And specifically, to our point: "When Paul wrote to the Philippians 'Whatever is true, whatever is honorable, whatever is just, whatever is pure, whatever is lovely, whatever is gracious, if there is any excellence, if there is anything worthy of praise, think about these things' (Phil. 4:8), he was only taking up a purely humanistic concept proper to that of philosophic wisdom." Pope Benedict XVI, *St. Paul* (San Francisco: Ignatius Press, 2017), 10–11.

in Nashville, Tennessee. The theme for that year was "Virtue in Our Current Culture: Living the Nobility of Strength and Goodness." My talk was on "St. Thomas Aquinas's Approach to Virtues and Vices" with a heavy emphasis on the seven deadly sins.

Now, this book did not grow from the material I prepared for that talk but from the scriptural verse from St. Paul that the Aquinas Forum used as a motto for that year's gathering: "Finally, brethren, whatever is true, whatever is honorable, whatever is just, whatever is pure, whatever is lovely, whatever is gracious, if there is any excellence, if there is anything worthy of praise, think about these things" (Phil. 4:8). Thinking about that verse is what, six years later, brought this book about.

What This Book Is About

This book is about taking St. Paul's words seriously and at face value—literally doing as he advised by carefully pondering each and every one of those things he told us were so worthy of thinking about—a chapter's worth for each "thing"! We will devote a chapter each to *truth*, *honor*, *justice*, *purity*, *loveliness*, *graciousness*, *excellence*, and *praiseworthy things*. In that sense, the book is not unlike the kind of "great ideas" the prominent twentieth-century Catholic psychologist and philosopher Mortimer Adler used to love to write and teach about; for example, in his *How to Think about the Great Ideas*.[2] Indeed, several of Paul's eight things, such as truth and justice, were included among Adler's great ideas.

[2] Mortimer J. Adler, *The Great Ideas: From the Great Books of Civilization* (Chicago: Open Court, 2000).

Here, though, we will have a few differences that make all the difference, since we will focus specifically on how these ideas were addressed by St. Paul as well as by his great commentators, foremost among them St. Thomas Aquinas (and of this, Adler, an ardent Thomist, would surely have approved!). As for the most important difference of all, in keeping with the intentions of St. Paul and St. Thomas, all these things will be considered in the light not only of the truth with a lowercase *t* but of Truth with a capital *T*: Jesus Christ, who is Himself "the way, and the truth, and the life" (John 14:6). As we consider these things, we will borrow many insights from the in-depth analyses of St. Thomas and of other saints and Church Fathers and from the richness of Scripture, from which they all gleaned their spiritual wisdom.

Our goal in this endeavor is that we might be better able to understand St. Paul's eight things, to climb his eight "steps" as we cast them, to happiness, holiness, and Heaven. Here, they are in brief. In the rest of this book, we will "think about these things" aplenty—so that we might *do* and *live* them!

Eight Things to Think About

> Finally brethren, whatever is true, whatever is honorable, whatever is just, whatever is pure, whatever is lovely, whatever is gracious, if there is any excellence, if there is anything worthy of praise, think about these things. (Phil. 4:8)

Below are St. Paul's eight "things" in the original Greek in which he wrote them, as they appear in the Latin Vulgate, in the Revised Standard Version of the Bible, Catholic Edition (RSVCE), and in the English Dominican Friars' translation of St. Thomas Aquinas's commentary on Paul's Letter to the Philippians.[3] Pondering the nuances of rich meaning in the various versions will give us plenty to think about.

Original Greek (transliterated)	**Latin Vulgate**	**Revised Standard Version, Catholic Edition**	**St. Thomas Aquinas's *Commentary on Philippians***
alethe	*vera*	true	true
semna	*pudica*	honorable	modest
dikaia	*justa*	just	just
hagna	*sancta*	pure	holy
prosphile	*amabilia*	lovely	lovely
euphema	*bonae famae*	gracious	of good fame
arete	*virtus*	excellence	virtue
epainos	*laus disciplinae*	worthy of praise	praise of discipline

[3] In St. Thomas Aquinas, *Commentary on the Letters of St. Paul to the Philippians, Colossians, Thessalonians, Timothy, Titus, and Philemon,* trans. F.R. Larcher, O.P., ed. J. Mortensen and E. Alcaron (Lader, WY: Aquinas Institute for the Study of Sacred Doctrine, 2012).

Eight Steps on a Stairway to Happiness, Holiness, and Heaven

Spiritual growth been described metaphorically in Scripture and by great saints as ascending a ladder, a staircase, a mountain, or a bridge and even going up in an elevator. Now, I don't know if an escalator has ever been suggested, and I'm not going to do so here, having settled upon a "stairway to Heaven." But first, let's look at a few great theological structures of spiritual ascent:

- Jacob "dreamed that there was a ladder set up on the earth, and the top of it reached to heaven; and behold, the angels of God were ascending and descending on it! And behold, the LORD stood above it" (Gen. 28:12–13).
- St. Benedict of Nursia (480–547), in his classic *Rule* for his monks, wrote of twelve degrees or steps toward the virtue of humility.
- Borrowing the imagery of Jacob's ladder, Eastern Church Father St. John Climacus (525–606) crafted his masterful work *The Ladder of Divine Ascent*. This spiritual ladder contains a full thirty-three steps of virtues to build and vices to conquer, each representing one year of Christ's life on earth. Climacus urges us, "Ascend my brothers, ascend eagerly. Let your heart's resolve be to climb!"
- St. Anselm of Canterbury (ca. 1033–1109), wrote of a seven-story mountain of humility in his *On Likeness* and *Dictums of Anselm*, encouraging all of us to ascend its steep path away from the dark valley of pride.
- St. Thomas Aquinas (ca. 1224–1274) wrote of three degrees of charity, the first step centering on conquering

sin, the second on growing in virtue, and the third on seeking union with God.[4]

- St. Catherine of Siena, in her "Treatise on Divine Providence" within her mystical *Dialogues*, wrote of Christ upon the Cross as our bridge to Heaven, as we ascend the steps at His feet, His side, and finally, His mouth.[5]
- Oh, and as for our elevator, St. Thérèse of Lisieux wrote in her autobiographical *Story of a Soul*: "I am determined to find an elevator to carry me to Jesus, for I was too small to climb the steep stairs of perfection, so I sought in Holy Scripture some idea of what this lift I wanted would be, and I read, 'Whoever is a little one, let him come to me' (Luke 8:16)."

While, to my knowledge, St. Paul did not use metaphors of climbing ladders, stairs, or mountains, and certainly not elevators or escalators, he did speak of stages of spiritual growth, telling us, for example: "When I was a child, I spoke like a child, I reasoned like a child; when I became a man, I gave up my childish ways" (1 Cor. 13:11). Further, regarding his brethren in Corinth, he wrote that because they were "men of the flesh," and "babes in Christ," he fed them "milk" at first (1 Cor. 3:1–2) because God wanted them to grow spiritually in "the mind of Christ" (1 Cor. 2:16). Here we will treat St.

4 St. Thomas Aquinas, *Summa Theologica*, II-II, q. 24, art. 9. Hereafter, references to the *Summa Theologica* [*ST*] will be given in parenthetical references in the text.

5 St. Catherine of Siena, *The Dialogue of St. Catherine of Siena*, trans. Algar Thorold (Charlotte, NC: Saint Benedict Press, 2006), 39–42.

Paul's "eight things" as a spiritual staircase of sorts, each step giving us more to reason maturely about, more spiritual food to chew on, as we learn, like St. Paul, to conform our minds to the mind of Christ.

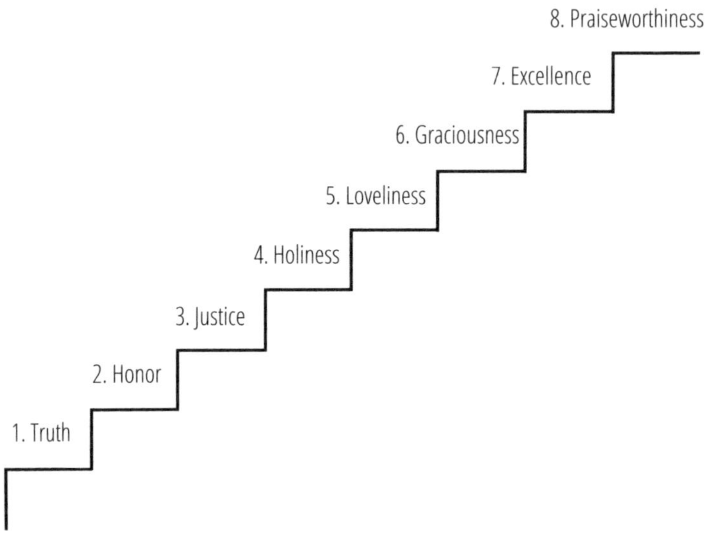

Let us take our first step and conclude this introduction with a spiritual appetizer.

The Angelic Doctor Always Helps Us Think about Things!

Whenever I need help thinking about things, after praying for God's guidance, my first stop is usually the writings of St. Thomas Aquinas, since he thought about so many things in such unparalleled depth. Now, did our Angelic Doctor provide a detailed analysis of this particular verse, Philippians 4:8, in his 1.8-million-word *Summa Theologica*? Well, not that I recall. Did he provide a detailed analysis elsewhere in his writings? You can rest assured that he certainly did, most fittingly in his aforementioned commentary on the letter to the Philippians.

Dipping into Philippians 4:9 as well, Thomas sums things up as follows:

> Then, when he says, "for the rest, brethren," he puts order into their activity by urging them to do good; first he mentions the object of action, namely, the good which is done; second, the mover to action; third, the act itself; fourth, the fruit of the act. These four things are mentioned here.[6]

Allow me to cull out in table form just a few of his insights on the nature of St. Paul's eight things of Philippians 4:8 and further elaborations in Philippians 4:9 using Thomas's translated words for them:

> Finally, brethren, whatever is true, whatever is honorable, whatever is just, whatever is pure, whatever is lovely, whatever is gracious, if there is any excellence, if there is anything worthy of praise, think about these things. What you have learned and received and heard and seen in me, do; and the God of peace will be with you. (Phil. 4:8–9)

[6] *Commentary on Philippians*, 62.

St. Paul's Eight Steps to Happiness

St. Thomas's Thoughts on Philippians 4:8–9

Object of the Intellect (Truth)	Objects of the Appetite (Good)	Good beyond What Is Necessary	Motiva-tors of Action	Fruits of the Acts
True	Modest (good in itself)	Lovely (leads to friendship)	Virtue (habits within us)	God: "The God of peace will be with you."
	Just (good directed to neighbor)	Gracious (leads to good reputation)	Praise of discipline (instruc-tion learned from someone else)	
	Holy (good directed to God)		Thinking (internal)	
			Doing (external)	

We will flesh out all these insights in the pages ahead. Hopefully, St. Thomas has whetted our appetites for plenty of food for thought as we get down to business, *thinking* deeply and widely about the very things St. Paul told us to, so that we might *do* them, attaining happiness, holiness, and eternal life in Heaven with the God of love and peace. Now it is almost time to take our first step toward the Truth that is also the way and the life—the Truth that sets us free. But first . . .

Eight More Things to Think About: "Think about This Saint [or Sage]" Chapter-End Essays

In response to a letter from a religious brother asking advice on how best to pursue his studies, among Thomas's many practical suggestions was this one: "Do not fail to imitate the lives of saintly and noble men."[7] Notice the inclusion of "noble" as well as saintly models for our lives. Some theologians in St. Thomas's day (the thirteenth century) were critical of his use of secular philosophy—that of Aristotle, in particular, but also of many others, including Socrates, Plato, and Seneca—in service of theology. They argued that he was diluting the wine of divine wisdom with the water of human wisdom. Thomas, however, knew that there is only one truth and that the truth of the Faith could never be contradicted by the truth of reason but that reason can help draw some people to the Faith and help clarify theological principles for the faithful. He did not believe that the noble philosophy of noble men diluted the faith whatsoever but, rather, that "those who use philosophical doctrines in sacred Scripture in such a way as to subject them

[7] See my book *How to Think Like Aquinas: The Sure Way to Perfect Your Mental Powers* (Manchester, NH: Sophia Institute Press, 2018), 61.

to the service of faith, do not mix water with wine, but change water into wine."[8]

Indeed, in subtle yet powerful ways, St. Paul did much the same, as when he appealed to the Greeks in Athens, revealing to them the "unknown god" their philosophy hinted at (Acts 17:23). When Paul explained to them about the true God, "'In him we live and move and have our own being'; as even some of your poets have said" (Acts 17:28), he was quoting from memory Epimenides of Crete of the seventh century B.C. Scholars have examined possible influences of Stoic ethical philosophy on the thought of St. Paul,[9] and, for centuries, a collection of letters circulated purporting to be correspondence between St. Paul and the Stoic philosopher Lucius Annaeus Seneca. While the letters have been found to be inauthentic, there is indeed a connection of sorts between Paul and Seneca within the Bible. When Paul was brought before the Roman proconsul of Achaia, who refused to judge him but referred him back to the Jews, that Roman official, Lucius Junius Gallio Annaeus, was Seneca's brother.

In these pages, we will follow St. Paul's and St. Thomas's leads in honoring both saintly and noble men (and indeed, women), by concluding each chapter with a brief essay, usually featuring a

8 See section 2.3, ad 5 in St. Thomas Aquinas, *Commentary on Boethius'* On the Trinity, St. Isidore Forum, https://isidore.co/aquinas/english/BoethiusDeTr.htm#L22.

9 For example, Troels Engberg-Pederson, *Paul and the Stoics* (Louisville, KY: Westminster John Knox Press, 2000). Moreover, Pope Benedict XVI, when discussing St. Paul, would declare: "We cannot gloss over certain names of its [Stoicism's] founders, Zeno and Cleanthes, and then those closer to Paul in time, such as Seneca, Musonius and Epictetus: in them the loftiest values of humanity and wisdom are found, which were naturally to be absorbed by Christianity." *St. Paul*, 10.

great *saint* but, in a couple of cases, a noble *sage* who embodied in his life and enhanced our understanding of the "thing" we examined in that chapter. These saints and sages should inspire us to live out our lives by their saintly and noble examples as we scale St. Paul's spiritual staircase to Heaven.

Let's begin by taking our first true step!

The Truth That Sets Us Free

If you continue in my word, you are truly my disciples, and you will know the truth, and the truth will make you free.

—John 8:31–32

Truth is the equation of thought and thing.

—St. Thomas Aquinas, *ST*, I, q. 16, art. 1

St. Thomas's Thoughts on Philippians 4:8–9

Object of the Intellect (Truth)	**Objects of the Appetite (Good)**	**Good beyond What Is Necessary**	**Motivators of Action**	**Fruits of the Acts**
True	Modest (good in itself)	Lovely (leads to friendship)	Virtue (habits within us)	God: "The God of peace will be with you."
	Just (good directed to neighbor)	Gracious (leads to good reputation)	Praise of discipline (instruction learned from someone else)	
	Holy (good directed to God)		Thinking (internal)	
			Doing (external)	

St. Paul	**Latin Vulgate**	**RSVCE**	**St. Thomas**
alethe	*vera*	true	true

St. Paul Sees the Light of Truth[10]

How ironic that when Pontius Pilate asked Jesus, "What is truth?" (John 18:38) and walked away without an answer, he had been staring Truth in the face! Indeed, Jesus had previously revealed to His disciples: "I am the way, and the truth, and the life" (John 14:6). As a Roman and simply as a human being, Pilate had the capacity to employ his natural reason to attain some partial truth about God—at least in that He exists. As St. Paul would later write to the Romans, the ungodly and wicked suppress the truth, but "what can be known about God is plain to them, because God has shown it to them. Ever since the creation of the world his invisible nature, namely, his eternal power and deity,

10 If you'll pardon the personal note, I find that God shows us His amazing timing and sense of humor. When asked by a priest of our diocese to record brief videos on each of the seven gifts of the Holy Spirit earlier this year, I decided to start each one with a story of a saint to illustrate each of the gifts. I had chosen St. Paul for the first gift—wonder and awe (also known as fear of the Lord)—and planned to tell the story of his conversion on the road to Damascus. As I approached my parish church, where we were to film, I was listening to a CD in my wife's car, and what should come on but the modern popular song "Suddenly I See!"

has been clearly perceived in that things that have been made" (Rom. 1:19–20). In our day, the *Catechism of the Catholic Church* (CCC) makes this point quite clearly: "By natural reason man can know God with certainty, on the basis of his works" (50). So the most important of truths, that God exists, is accessible to every person willing to employ his powers of observation and reason.

Young Saul of Tarsus (ca. 5–ca. 64), a Roman citizen, knew this truth of natural reason. As a member of the Hebrew race, he knew the source of all truth at a far deeper level. God chose to reveal Himself to Moses on Mount Sinai as the great "YHWH," the great "I AM," being itself, the eternal source and sustainer of all that is and yet also "the God of Abraham, the God of Isaac, and the God of Jacob" (Exod. 3:14–15).

Saul, however, did *not* believe God's newer and deeper revelation that came to us through His own Son, the Word Incarnate, Jesus Christ, who declared, like the voice from the burning bush, that "before Abraham was, I am" (John 8:58). Saul believed that the "Nazarenes" who followed the deceased Jesus of Nazareth were heretics who merited imprisonment and even death. When the first Christian martyr, Stephen, was stoned and prayed to God for mercy on his killers with his dying breath, "Saul was consenting to his death" (Acts 8:1). Soon after, Saul "laid waste the church, and entering house after house, he dragged off men and women and committed them to prison" (Acts 8:3).

Of course, a very unusual thing happened to Saul on the road to Damascus to persecute more Christians, as he was suddenly knocked off his high horse, so to speak.[11] Here is what we know for sure about the first moments of this miraculous event:

[11] Although artistic and cinematic presentations depict Saul falling off his horse, which seems very likely, Scripture does not

> As he journeyed he approached Damascus, and suddenly a light from heaven flashed about him. And he fell to the ground and heard a voice saying to him, "Saul, Saul, why do you persecute me? And he said, "Who are you, Lord?" And he said, "I am Jesus, whom you are persecuting; but rise and enter the city, and you will be told what you are to do." (Acts 9:3–6)

Saul's companions heard the voice too but saw no one. When Saul arose, he realized he could see nothing at all, and being led by hand to Damascus, he remained blind for three days. Meanwhile, God spoke to a Christian in the city named Ananias and told him to seek out Saul and to restore his sight in God's name. Ananias, hesitant at first, knowing Saul's terrifying reputation, obeyed the Lord and entered the place where Saul was staying. Here is what happened next:

> Laying his hands on him [Ananias] said, "Brother Saul, the Lord Jesus who appeared to you on the road by which you came, has sent me that you may regain your sight and be filled with the Holy Spirit." And immediately something like scales fell from his eyes and he regained his sight. Then he rose and was baptized, and took food and was strengthened. (Acts 9:17–19)

Well, Saul and the rest of the world have not been quite the same since, thanks be to God! Paul had literally seen the light and heard the voice of the One who is the truth, and the way,

---

explicitly say this. For a famous striking example, see Caravaggio's 1601 masterpiece *The Conversion of St. Paul on the Road to Damascus*.

and the life, and he would devote the rest of his life to learning and spreading the truth of the gospel of Jesus Christ. He would become the Apostle[12] to the Gentiles, adopting the Romanized name Paul, meaning, as we noted, "small," perhaps to counter his intimidating reputation as the great persecutor Saul! We'll see more of Paul's life and his lessons in the pages ahead, but now let us move toward a deeper examination of truth from a human perspective, since Paul advised us to think about truth so that we might live by it.

Truth from the Human Perspective—and as It Exists in God

The atheistic philosopher Friedrich Nietzsche infamously wrote in his *Thus Spoke Zarathustra*: "This is my way, where is yours—thus I answered those who asked me 'the way.' For the way—that does not exist." How sad that the son of a Lutheran minister, who had died when Friedrich had not yet reached age five, did not believe that there was indeed "the way," whose name is Jesus Christ. In our day, many people hold the same attitude toward *truth itself*, believing effectively, "This is my truth, where is yours? For 'the truth'—that does not exist." This popular idea that there is no absolute truth, but only truth relative to one's perspective, is called *relativism*.

Pope Benedict XVI had warned in 2005: "We are building a dictatorship of relativism that does not recognize anything as definitive and whose ultimate good consists solely of one's own

[12] Recall that St. Thomas Aquinas's honorific name for St. Paul in the *Summa Theologica* is simply "the Apostle"; and the great Franciscan St. Bonaventure likewise used that name.

ego and desires."[13] Indeed, his warning came in his commentary on a reading from St. Paul's Letter to the Ephesians (4:14–15) in which Paul warns us not to be like children "tossed to and fro and carried about with every wind of doctrine," by the cunning of deceitful people, but, rather, to go forth "speaking the truth in love," growing "up in every way into him who is the head, into Christ."

It is plain to see how what Paul and Benedict warned about has come to pass in the most egregious ways in merely the last handful of years; for example, some people, in order to satisfy their own ego and desires, believe not only that their own biological sex is not definitive and true but that others must be compelled to affirm "their truth" about such matters. The Church, however, has understood the true nature of truth itself, through solid doctrine taught across the millennia. When St. Thomas Aquinas addressed the essence of God as truth itself, he also provided several statements from various theologians and philosophers on the nature of truth from a human perspective. Here are some examples:

- Augustine of Hippo: "Truth is that whereby is made manifest that which is" (*De Vera Relig.* 36).
- Hilary of Poitiers: "Truth makes being clear and evident" (*De Trin.* 5).
- Anselm of Canterbury: "Truth is rightness, perceptible by the mind alone" (*De Verit.* 12).
- Avicenna (the Persian philosopher Ibn Sina): "The truth of each thing is a property of the essence which is immutably attached to it" (*Metaph.* 8, 6).

[13] Joseph Cardinal Ratzinger, homily at the Vatican basilica, April 18, 2005, https://www.vatican.va/gpII/documents/homily-pro-eligendo-pontifice_20050418_en.html.

Please note two important elements among the various definitions of truth: (1) some *thing* that actually *is*—"being," "rightness," "essence"—(2) is comprehended in *thought* as it is "made manifest," "clear and evident," "perceptible by the mind alone." Hence, we arrive at Thomas's own pithy definition: "Truth is the equation of thought and thing."[14]

We seem to live in an age that has forgotten the truth of the old aphorism "Thinking doesn't make it so." Shakespeare did write in *Hamlet*, "There is nothing either good or bad, but thinking makes it so." We can indeed change our thoughts and attitudes about things, and this can alter our emotions and behaviors. This is a cornerstone of Stoic philosophy and modern cognitive psychotherapy. Still, our thoughts alone do not change external reality. Indeed, I would confidently wager that people who argue the contrary, that the power of human thought alone can indeed override external reality, still look both ways before crossing the street! (Who among us has ever had much success in thinking away a Mack truck?)

So seeking the truth does indeed mean that we must seek to conform our thoughts with the facts of external reality. The scientific method for finding truths about the material world looks for cause-and-effect relationships that do, in fact, exist—whether we like them or not!

Consider for just a moment the philosophical and scriptural teaching on the "intellectual virtues" of science or knowledge (*science* deriving from the Latin *scire*—"to know"), understanding, and wisdom. They can be found in Aristotle's ethical treatises and in Scripture as well; for example, "By wisdom a house is built, and

14 All drawn from *ST*, I, q. 16, art. 1, "Whether Truth Resides Only in the Intellect?"

by understanding it is established; by knowledge the rooms are filled with all precious and pleasant riches" (Prov. 24:3–4). God Himself manifests them in the creation of the world: "The LORD by wisdom founded the earth; by understanding he established the heavens; by his knowledge the deeps broke forth, and the clouds drop down the dew" (Prov. 3:19–20). Borrowing form St. Thomas, the intellectual virtues can be tersely defined as follows:

Science or knowledge pertains to the comprehension of cause-and-effect relationships.

Understanding pertains to the grasp of fundamental, underlying principles.

Wisdom pertains to the judgments made regarding the highest of causes and the most fundamental of principles.

St. Thomas described their relationship like this: "Science depends on understanding as on a virtue of higher degree: and both of these depend on wisdom, as obtaining the highest place, and containing beneath itself understanding and science, by judging both the conclusions of science, and of the principles on which they are based" (*ST*, I, q. 57, art. 2).

When these three develop within us *as virtues*, we become better able to use our reasoning powers to grasp deeper and more important truths. God, being infinitely generous and gracious, has also graced us with three *gifts of the Holy Spirit*—namely, knowledge, understanding, and wisdom—that further perfect these intellectual powers, making them amenable not merely to the limited powers of human intellect but to the stirrings of the all-knowing, infallible Holy Spirit, helping us to comprehend and judge things from God's perspective as well as our own.[15]

[15] For more on all seven gifts of the Holy Spirit, see Isaiah 11:1–3 for their scriptural origin, CCC 1831, Thomas's extensive

Scripture tells us that God is the ultimate source of science, understanding, and wisdom. For example: "For the LORD gives wisdom; from his mouth come knowledge and understanding" (Prov. 2:6). This might lead to a question: What, then, is truth from *God's* perspective?

Recall that "Our Lord says, *I am the Way, the Truth, and the Life* (John 14:6)" (*ST*, I, q. 16, art. 5). We have seen that Thomas told us that truth, from the human perspective, is the correspondence between reality and our mental grasp of it, conformity between thing and thought. Well, not only do created things conform or correspond to God's thought, but "His act of understanding is the measure and cause of every other being and intellect." Truth does not merely exist in God, as it can in us, but "He is truth itself, and the sovereign and first truth" (*ST*, I, q. 16, art. 5). For us, thinking does not make it so. For God, it does!

Living the Virtue of Truth in Our Lives

There are many more truths about truth that are truly worth thinking about. St. Thomas Aquinas begins with two fundamental senses of *veritas*, or truth:

1. That by reason of which a thing is said to be true, *the object or end of a virtue*: "a certain equality between the understanding or sign and the thing understood, or again between a thing and its rule."
2. "Truth may stand for that by which a person says what is true, in which sense one is said to be truthful. This

---

treatment of each one, scattered throughout *ST*, II, or my own *Seven Gifts of the Holy Spirit* (Sophia Institute Press, 2016). We will also examine them in a little more depth in this book's chapter 8 and the intellectual virtues in chapter 7.

> truth or *truthfulness must needs be a virtue*, because to say what is true is a good act; and virtue is 'that which makes its possessor good, and renders his action good.'"

Meaning number 1 is what we've been talking about. Truth from the human perspective is the correspondence between thought and thing. Meaning number 2 addresses how we practice truth in our lives. Truth lived, or *truthfulness*, is the correspondence between thought and word or action. As Thomas cited the words of the Roman philosopher Cicero, by "truth we faithfully represent things as they are, were, or will be." We are called to build the habit or virtue of truth within ourselves so that we always speak what we know to be true.

Thomas spells out the nature of truth in the eight articles of the *Summa Theologica*, part I, question 16, "Of Truth," as he explores the divine attributes of God. His bottom-line conclusions are as follows:

1. Truth is the equation of thought and thing, residing primarily in the intellect and secondarily in things.
2. Truth resides in the mind of man through his reasoning processes, but simply and completely in the mind of God.
3. *Truth* is a convertible or interchangeable term with *being* in reality, but they do differ in idea, truth residing primarily in the intellect and being residing primarily in things. (All things that are true exist, though there are nuances in meaning in the way we use the words *truth* and *being* or *existence*.)
4. Truth is logically prior to the good within the intellect. (We recognize simply that a thing truly exists before we assess its value.)

5. Truth is God—or more properly arranged, God is truth.
6. Truth is many within the minds of created intellectual beings, but one according to the primary truth of the divine intellect.
7. Truth is eternal as it exists in the mind of God.
8. Truth can change in the minds of creatures, but it is immutable in the mind of God.[16]

Thomas returns to look at truth in its second meaning more than fifteen hundred pages later in the *Summa* in the four articles of part II-II, question 109, "Of Truth." Here, he examines truth or truthfulness as it is lived out in human thoughts, words, and deeds. As for his bottom-line summaries:

1. Truth is a virtue.
2. Truth is a special virtue.
3. Truth is a part of justice.
4. Truth is more defiled by exaggeration than by understatement.

Now let's look at the truths that rest above those bottom lines.

Truth Is a Virtue

Truth's nature *as a virtue* means that it is a habit, a disposition we build in ourselves to tell what we believe to be the truth. Thomas notes that Aristotle, the great Greek philosopher Thomas honors with the title "the Philosopher" in the *Summa*, lists truth as a virtue in both the second and fourth books of his great *Nicomachean*

[16] As summarized in my book *What Is God? Answering the World's Most Important Question with Help from Thomas Aquinas* (El Cajon, CA: Catholic Answers Press, 2022), 166. See that book's chapter 16 or *ST*, I, q. 16, if you'd care for more detailed explanations.

Ethics, a wonderful treatise on which Thomas wrote his own commentary, addressing the meaning of every single line![17] Further, quoting Aristotle, "truth or truthfulness is a good act; and virtue is *that which makes its possessor good, and renders his action good.*"

Aristotle is also famous for describing virtues as embodying "golden means," hitting the precise mark of neither excess nor deficiency, neither too much nor too little, to achieve the golden peak of excellence. For example, regarding acts of bravery prompted by fortitude or courage, too little fortitude would imply timidity or fearfulness, whereas too much could entail foolhardy temerity that could lead one unnecessarily into dangerous situations.

Thomas notes that truthfulness is a moral virtue with its own golden mean, which can be seen in two ways. The first way relates to *the object of truth*, "because the true essentially denotes a kind of equality, and equal is a mean between more and less." So when a person says what is true about himself, he observes the mean by saying neither more nor less than what is true about himself, neither exaggerating nor understating things. The second way relates to *the act of truth*. Here, observing the mean means "to tell the truth, when one ought, and as one ought. Excess consists in making known one's affairs out of season and deficiency in hiding them when one ought to make them known." As for the excess, perhaps you are familiar with the acronym TMI for "too much information," or the sarcastic remark "Thank you for sharing that!" when someone has related some delicate fact that would have been better left unsaid. As for the deficiency of truth, see the nightly news reporting on just about any scandal and cover-up.

[17] St. Thomas Aquinas, *Commentary on Aristotle's* Nicomachean Ethics, trans. C. I. Litzinger, O.P. (Notre Dame, IN: Dumb Ox Books, 1993).

Truth Is a Special Virtue

As for this business about truth as a *special virtue*, Thomas notes that some people argued that truth is not really a unique or special virtue. They said, for example, that to declare or make known real things about oneself is an act of truth, but every virtue works this way, "since every virtuous habit is made known by its own act" (e.g., fortitude is shown by brave acts, temperance by acts of self-control). Therefore, truth is not a unique virtue but an element of every virtue.

Thomas notes, to the contrary, however, building upon insights from St. Augustine, that there is also a special act that is uniquely under the province of truth—namely, "a special order whereby our externals, whether words or deeds, are duly ordered in relation to some thing, as sign to thing signified; and thereto man is perfected by the virtue of truth. Wherefore it is evident that truth is a special virtue." In other words, truth is not only a generic aspect of every virtue, but truth has earned its own unique spot on the roll call of moral virtues!

Truth Serves Justice

And exactly where does truth's name lie on that esteemed list of virtues? As we will explore in some depth when we come to chapters 3 and 7, St. Thomas has provided a delightfully thorough way of classifying every moral virtue, highlighting three classes of "parts" or related virtues that accompany the four cardinal virtues of fortitude, temperance, justice, and prudence. For now, let us know that Thomas assigns truth its place as a part of *justice*.

We'll do justice, well, justice, so to speak, when we come to chapter 3, but for now, we will simply note that justice, at its core, involves giving others their rightful due. Now, the virtue of truth has two important things in common with the virtue of justice. First, truth, in the sense of truthfulness, is also a *social* virtue, being directed toward others by sharing with them truths about the things that concern them. Second, justice sets up a kind of *equality* between things, and the virtue of truth does too, "for it equals signs to the things which concern man himself"; that is, it makes sure that our words accurately represent the things we proclaim to others. Whereas justice regards legal debts we owe one another, truth regards "moral debt," in that we owe one another the truth. Thomas emphasizes, echoing Aristotle, that we are social animals and that we owe one another whatever is required to preserve human society. It would be impossible for people to live together in peace unless they believed one another. As Christ told us, "Whatever you wish that men would do to you, do so to them" (Matt. 7:12; cf. Luke 6:31). No one wants to be lied to, and neither should we lie to other people. Truth clearly serves the cardinal virtue of justice and Christian love as well.

Truth Is More Defiled by Exaggeration Than by Understatement

What do we mean by saying that truth is more defiled by exaggeration than by understatement? Good question. Let's turn to the Angelic Doctor and the Philosopher for the answer. Thomas's heading of his fourth article on truth is "Whether the Virtue of Truth Inclines Rather to That Which Is Less?" Thomas borrows here from Aristotle, who wrote that while every moral virtue consists in a golden mean, it also "inclines to"—or is, in a sense, nearer to—one of the two vices on either side of it in terms of deficiency or excess. For example, if we think of the virtue of prudence or practical wisdom, we tend first to think of the most offending contrary vice that is the deficiency of wisdom, which is foolishness. The book of Proverbs can be mined for many verses contrasting the wise person with the fool, one of the most graphic (and my favorite) being that the wise person "lay[s] up knowledge," whereas the fool repeats his folly "like a dog that returns to his vomit" (Prov. 10:14; 26:11). The vice contrary to prudence in terms of excess could be called craftiness or cunning, in which a person uses successful means to achieve his goals, but the goal and the means are deceptive and hurtful to others.[18]

In this analysis of truthfulness, Thomas agrees with Aristotle that in untruths regarding ourselves, it defiles truth less, or is a less egregious offense against truth, to understate or play things down than to boast or exaggerate about oneself. For one thing, those who boast about themselves annoy other people because they seem to strive to outstrip or one-up others, whereas those who make less of themselves often provide pleasure to others, since they seem to defer to them by their restraint and moderation. Indeed, we may see this tendency in the wise and learned and in holy people who may tend to downplay their own capacities or achievements for the sake of others. So, while truthfulness about oneself is indeed the golden mean of the virtue of truth, "it is more repugnant to prudence to think or boast that one has what one has not, than to think or say that one has not what one has."

[18] I happen to be writing just at the time when a person has been arrested for allegedly causing great financial harm to others by a massive Ponzi scheme involving cryptocurrency. It might turn out that a person considered amazingly prudent may have actually been far more crafty or cunning, and then truth caught up with him.

Three Kinds of Sin against Truth: Lying, Hypocrisy, and Boasting and Its Opposite

Truth sets us free, while untruths chain us in webs of our own deceit. After considering the virtue of truth, Thomas addresses three questions, totaling ten articles, on three vices that oppose truthfulness—namely, lying, hypocrisy, and boasting and its opposite (i.e., irony). Thomas makes clear that all forms of lying oppose the virtue of truth, and he also lays out an intriguing analysis of the nature of lies and the various forms they assume.

Two Ways to Classify Lies

Their Nature as Lies (per Aristotle)	Their Nature as Sins (per gloss on Psalm 5:7[6])
Boasting	Jocular
Irony	Officious
	Mischievous

Thomas says that Aristotle rightly describes *boasting* as a lie that exceeds the mean of truth, whereas *irony* is a lie "which falls short of the truth by saying something less."

Thomas next addresses a gloss[19] on Psalm 5:7 in the Vulgate, or Psalm 5:6 in the RSVCE, which reads in the latter: "Thou destroyest those who speak lies." The gloss refers to three kinds

[19] The *Glossa Ordinaria*, widely used in the Middle Ages, was a version of the Latin Vulgate Bible whose margins contained brief glosses (comments or explanations) compiled from the writings of various Church Fathers.

of lies: (1) those told "for the well-being and convenience of someone," (2) those told "for fun," and (3) those told "out of malice." They are, in the language of our table, *jocular* lies (told in jest as jokes), *officious* lies (told to help or to spare another from harm), and *mischievous* lies (told to injure another). Thomas says these refer to lies in their nature as *sins*, and as you might surmise, Thomas holds mischievous, intentionally harmful lies as the most grievous kind.

But what of lies in the form of jokes, or lies intended to help a person, as when a physician or a family member might withhold a dire medical diagnosis, at least for a time, from a person who may be psychologically fragile? Thomas cites Augustine, who argues that every form of lie opposes the virtue of truth, and yet he is certainly aware that there can be attenuating circumstances and that not every lie is a mortal sin.

As for joking, a story is told that some of Thomas's religious brethren once pranked him while he was studying, calling him to the window to see some pigs flying about outside. When Thomas came to the window and saw no pigs, he responded amid their laughter that he would rather believe that pigs could fly than that his Dominican brethren could lie! Still, we do know for sure that Thomas could appreciate humor and lightheartedness. As he wrote elsewhere (*ST*, II-II, q. 168, art. 4): "In human affairs whatever is against reason is a sin. Now it is against reason for a man to be burdensome to others, and by hindering their enjoyment." Further, "a man who is without mirth, not only is lacking playful speech, but is also burdensome to others, since he is deaf to the moderate mirth of others."

Thomas's deepest concern is for malicious, mischievous lies, affronts to truth that are told to produce harm. These are the lies that can be mortal sins if their subject matter is grave and if they are told with the liar's full knowledge and deliberate and complete consent. May the virtue of truth spare us from such soul-destroying vicious lies!

Three Arrows That Miss the Bull's-Eye of Truth

Aristotle wrote that there are many vices that can miss the mark of a virtue, just as there are many ways that arrows can miss a target's bull's-eye. Three other vices that miss the bull's-eye of truth are *hypocrisy*, and as we touched on briefly above, *boasting* and *irony*, or what we might call a false humility.

Thomas, drawing on the wisdom of the seventh-century scholar St. Isidore of Seville, was quite aware that hypocrisy derives from the Greek word *hypokrites*, which means "actor." As an actor puts on a mask to pretend he is someone other than himself, so does a hypocrite present a false image to the world by pretending to be what he is not. Hypocrisy is a direct affront to truth, whereby one tries to deceive others by pretending to possess a virtuous character or a holiness that he lacks. It may or may not be a mortal sin. Thomas, as usual, swiftly gets to the heart of the matter. Hypocrisy consists of two things: "lack of holiness, and simulation thereof." If a hypocrite does not care about holiness but only wants to appear holy to others, it is a mortal sin. We might recall, as well, Jesus' own admonishment: "Woe to you, scribes and Pharisees, hypocrites! For you are like whitewashed tombs, which outwardly appear beautiful, but within they are full of dead men's bones and all uncleanness. So you also outwardly appear righteous to men, but within you are full of hypocrisy and iniquity" (Matt. 23:27–28).

On the other hand, the intention to appear good, without disdain for holiness itself, "is not contrary to charity" and is not itself a mortal sin. Further, Gregory the Great has noted that hypocrisy is born out of the sin of vainglory, which is not always a mortal sin. In either case, however, hypocrisy is an affront to truth, and if we are to heed St. Paul's advice to think about truth, we will think as well about avoiding all forms of hypocrisy.

Two other arrows that miss truth's mark are boasting and irony. The *boasting* that exceeds the mean of truth to glorify oneself or achieve profit for oneself can become a mortal sin when it is contrary to charity, as

> when a man boasts of that which is contrary to God's glory—thus it is said in the person of the king of Tyre (Ezek. 28:2): "Thy heart is lifted up, and thou hast said: I am God," or contrary to the love of our neighbor, as when a man while boasting of himself belittles others, like the Pharisee who said, "I am not as the rest of men, extortioners, unjust, adulterers, as also is this publican" (Luke 18:11). According to the Psalms, "The boastful may not stand before my eyes" (Ps. 5:5).

Boasting is a venial sin when someone boasts of things that do not oppose God or harm his neighbor.

Finally, as for *irony*, or understating the truth about oneself, we can also look upon it as a kind of false humility. In the eloquent words of Augustine: "If thou liest on account of humility, if thou wert not a sinner before lying, then thou hast become one by lying." The truly humble certainly do not boast, exaggerating their capacities or their good qualities of character, but neither do they offend against truth by belittling themselves through pretending not to possess some good qualities they do indeed possess. Indeed, Augustine would also write: "Shun not arrogance so as to forsake truth," and Gregory the Great chimes in that it "is a reckless humility that entangles itself with lies."

In general, irony is a less grievous sin than boasting, since boasting often makes one disagreeable to others, while irony is often expressed by those who do not want to be disagreeable to others, perhaps by inciting their envy. Building upon Scripture, Aristotle, and Augustine, Thomas also warns against the kind of ironic self-belittlement that some people express "to make a show of some spiritual excellence." Jesus spoke of people who "disfigure their faces that their fasting may be seen by men" (Matt. 6:16). Aristotle said, "It is the practice of boasters ... to make very little of themselves," and it was for this reason that Augustine "was unwilling to possess clothes that were either too costly or too shabby, because by both do men seek glory." Indeed, we also read in Scripture: "There is one that humbleth himself wickedly, and his interior is full of deceit" (Ecclus. 19:23, D-R).[20]

[20] In the RSVCE, this would appear to be Sirach 19:26: "There is a rascal bowed down in mourning, but inwardly he is full of deceit."

Summing Up Step 1: Truth

St. Paul advised us to think about whatever is *alethe*, *vera*—true. Well, we have begun to think about truth in the light of Jesus Christ, who is truth. Through the insights of St. Thomas Aquinas, St. Augustine, Aristotle, and other great theologians and philosophers, we have thought deeply about the truth that God is in His essence, the truth that is the correspondence between thought and thing, and the truth that exists within our souls as a special and powerful virtue that helps us live in the image and likeness of the God who is truth who created us and sustains us. We have thought about perils to truth in our time and in all times, from the errors of moral relativism to the sins of lying, hypocrisy, boasting, and even selling ourselves short through false humility. Hopefully, this has given us even more to think about regarding truth. For those who might care to dig deeper into the Angelic Doctor's thoughts about truth, see *Summa Theologica*, I, question 16, "Of Truth," regarding truth as a divine attribute of God, and II-II, questions 109, "Of Truth"; 110, "Of the Vice Opposed to Truth, and First of Lying"; 111, "Of Dissimulation and Hypocrisy"; 112, "Of Boasting"; and 113, "Of Irony."

Next, we will take our second step up St. Paul's staircase to happiness, holiness, and Heaven, as we think about whatever is *semna*, *pudica*, honorable, or modest.

Think about This Saint #1

Dominic de Guzman (1170-1221)

Veritas.

—Motto of the Dominican Order

From where I sit as I type, I can see a bronze statue of a man in a religious habit holding an open Bible in his left hand and raising his right hand as if caught in the act of preaching. At his side, oddly enough, is a dog with a torch in its mouth. Well, there's really nothing odd about any of that, for the man is Dominic de Guzman, well versed in Scripture and the founder of the Order of Preachers. Before he was born, his mother, Bl. Jane of Aza, had a vision in which she gave birth to a dog carrying a torch in its mouth to set the world aflame. Well, her son Dominic would go on to form the Order of Preachers, also known as the Dominicans, which prompted a medieval pun upon their name as the "hounds [or dogs] of the Lord" from the Latin *domini* (of the Lord) and *canis* (hound or dog). The Dominicans would become known for spreading the light of Christ's gospel all around the world. (Indeed, a group of Dominican Sisters lives barely a mile down the road from me in Central Illinois.)

Dominic lived very much in the spirit of St. Paul with an unquenched zeal for spreading Christ's gospel. In his day, that of the early thirteenth century, the Albigensian heresy, which taught, among other things, that all of material creation, including the body, was evil, was spreading throughout Southern France. According to one of the early anecdotes about Dominic's life, he spent an entire night in conversation with an innkeeper, drawing him back to the Catholic Faith by morning. Seeing that many people were impressed by the simple lives of the preachers of the heresy, contrasted with the rich opulence of many bishops and priests who tried to dissuade them, Dominic formed the Order of Preachers with vows of humility, obedience, and poverty, which helped win back many heretics to the Church. Indeed, he founded his itinerant preachers at nearly the same time his colleague St. Francis founded his Order of Friars Minor (the Franciscans), and both did great work to restore the Church.

Unlike monks who lived in monasteries, taking a vow of stability, or priests who were tied to parishes, Dominic's preachers would be itinerants, wandering about both cities and countrysides, spreading the word of Christ near and far. Of special relevance to our chapter on truth, *Veritas*, truth itself, would become a motto of the Order of Preachers. They praised and practiced *study*, which, along with *preaching*, *prayer*, and *community* life, would become known as their four pillars. The order would attract and form great saints known for their wisdom and love of truth, including three great Church Doctors: St. Albert the Great, patron saint of scientists; St. Thomas Aquinas, patron saint of scholars; and St. Catherine of Siena, patron saint of nurses.

May we all come to love the truth like Dominic and grow in zeal to spread Christ's gospel. His feast day is August 8. St. Dominic de Guzman, pray for us!

Honoring the Honorable

Great are the works of the LORD, studied by all who have pleasure in them. Full of honor and majesty is his work.

—Psalm 111:2–3

Love one another with brotherly affection;
outdo one another in showing honor.

—Romans 12:10

St. Thomas's Thoughts on Philippians 4:8–9

Object of the Intellect (Truth)	***Objects of the Appetite (Good)***	Good beyond What Is Necessary	Motivators of Action	Fruits of the Acts
True	***Modest (good in itself)***	Lovely (leads to friendship)	Virtue (habits within us)	God: "The God of peace will be with you."
	Just (good directed to neighbor)	Gracious (leads to good reputation)	Praise of discipline (instruction learned from someone else)	
	Holy (good directed to God)		Thinking (internal)	
			Doing (external)	

St. Paul	Latin Vulgate	RSVCE	St. Thomas
semna	*pudica*	honorable	modest

St. Paul Bids Us to Honor Honorable Things

After telling us in Philippians to think about whatever is *alethe* (true), Paul adds that we should think about whatever is *semna* as our next step. Many English translations of the Bible, such as the RSVCE, translate *semna* (from the Greek *semnos*) as "honorable," while other versions render it as "honest," "noble," "admirable," or "respectable," all synonyms for the same fundamental meaning Paul had in mind. The Douay-Rheims translates the Latin word *pudica* into English as "modest," as does St. Thomas Aquinas in his commentary on Philippians. A modern dictionary of classical Greek gives other English words for *semnos*, including "august," "sacred," and "dignified," among other options.[21] The different nuances of the English words used to translate *semna* might well give us food for thought, but here we will focus primarily upon whatever is "honorable," and near the end, in a nod to Sts. Jerome (translator of the Latin Vulgate Bible) and Thomas Aquinas, we will think about modesty too.

Those who thoughtfully read Scripture will find plenty of chances to think about whatever is honorable. A modern biblical

[21] Dr. Karl Feyerabend, *Langenscheidt's Pocket Dictionary: Classical Greek-English* (Langenscheidt: Berlin, n.d.), 342.

concordance cites 199 references to *honor*, 11 to *honorable*, 3 to *honorably*, 56 to *honored*, 4 to *honoring*, and 14 to *honors*.[22] Though we'll address the smallest fraction of those 287 citations (if I've done my math right), we have plenty to think about and had better get busy.

What Is Most Worthy of Honor?

"What" is most worthy of honor and respect is actually a "Who." God, as goodness itself and the Creator of every other good that exists, is certainly most worthy of our honor in a way that no mere creature is. The special way in which we honor the three Persons of the Holy Trinity alone is called *latria* in Latin, from the Greek *latreia*, meaning "worship" or "adoration" in English. St. Thomas lays it out like this:

> Since servant implies relation to a lord, wherever there is a special kind of lordship there must needs be a special kind of service. Now it is evident that lordship belongs to God in a special and singular way, because He made all things, and has supreme dominion over all. Consequently a special kind of service is due to Him, which is known as *latria* [*latreia*] in the Greek; and therefore it belongs to religion. (*ST*, II-II, q. 81, art. 1)

Let's note that Thomas considers latria here in the context of his discussion of *religion as a virtue*, a habit we build in our souls to render God His rightful due within the limits of our

[22] *The Catholic Bible Concordance, Revised Standard Version, Catholic Edition*, comp. C. W. Lyons with Thomas Deliduka (Steubenville, OH: Emmaus Road Publishing, 2008), 846–848.

powers. Thomas tells us that when the psalmist writes, "My heart and flesh sing for joy to living God" (84:2), he refers to internal actions belonging to the heart and external actions belonging to the members of our flesh. The virtue of religion, therefore, includes *interior acts* of devotion and prayer as well as *exterior acts* of adoration, sacrifice, oblations, and first-fruits, tithes, vows, and oaths.

Now, while latria, the supreme honor of worship and adoration, belongs to God alone, recall the words from the psalmist that started our chapter: "Great are the works of the LORD, studied by all who have pleasure in them. Full of honor and majesty is his work" (111:2–3). When we honor and show our gratitude for the majestic works of creation, we thereby honor the Creator even more so. "For from the greatness and beauty of created things comes a corresponding perception of their Creator" (Wisd. 13:5). St. Thomas has conveyed this idea with awe-inspiring insight:

> He produced many and diverse creatures, that what was wanting to one in the representation of the divine goodness might be supplied by another. For goodness, which in God is simple and uniform, in creatures is manifold and divided, and hence the whole universe together participates in the divine goodness more perfectly, and represents it better than any single creature. (*ST*, I, q. 47. art. 1)

Recalling Thomas's analysis of Paul's eight things from our introduction, in the *true*, we treat of the object of the intellect, and in the *honorable*, we move to the first of three objects of our appetites, and we desire that which is good. The first good, that which is honorable, is that which is good in itself. Thomas tells us that God is goodness itself and that everything He creates participates in His goodness within its own essence, in a limited way. Therefore, we are to honor God above all but also to give due honor to all creation, being good stewards as we exercise dominion over all the things of the earth (Gen. 1:26–30; 2:15). We are utterly surrounded by good things worthy of our honor. Think about it!

Honoring Our Parents, Our Nation, and the Communion of Saints

The unique honor we owe to God is expressed in the first three of the Ten Commandments God gave to Moses: to worship God alone and no false gods, not to use the Lord's name in vain, and to honor the Sabbath Day (Exod. 20:2–17; Deut. 5:6–21). In the very next commandment, we are told to honor our fathers and our mothers. The *virtue* by which we show this honor to our parents is called *piety*. St. Thomas explains that piety also extends to the honor due to one's country, called one's fatherland or motherland in many nations. Why? Per Thomas: "Man is debtor chiefly to his parents and his country, after God" (*ST*, II-II, q. 101, art. 1).

We are protected, nurtured, and trained by our parents when we are completely helpless without them, and we do so within the auspices of the broader community of the nation in which we are raised. We can never completely repay the inestimable debt we owe to our parents, but through showing them honor, we do so to the best of our abilities. Such honor is demonstrated by outward displays of respect for our parents, by seeking regular contact with them, by listening to them, and by helping to care for their needs if they should become helpless late in life or at any time, due to injury or disease. We honor our nation by obeying its just laws and fulfilling all the legitimate duties of good citizens. A proper patriotic nationalism is indeed a virtuous thing, and such honor of one's country does not imply dishonor to the countries of others.

We might ask ourselves if we have thought much lately of how we can show honor to our parents, perhaps by a simple visit or a phone call if they are alive, or perhaps by a prayer or a Mass for them or a visit to their graves if they are deceased. We might ask ourselves as well if we have honored our nation, perhaps by acts as simple as taking the trouble to do our part to ensure that the most honorable people, truly devoted to the common good, are elected to offices of power.

There is also another, higher form of piety, for we belong to a heavenly family as well as to an earthly one. Through the Holy Spirit's *gift of piety*, we receive the Holy Spirit's inspiration to honor God not only as our Creator and sustainer but as Father to us all. Indeed, every Christian should know that the Son called us to this kind of piety in the very first words He taught us about how we should pray: "Our Father" (Matt. 6:9; cf. Luke 11:2). As adopted children of God through Christ, we all become members of God's family—brothers and sisters in Christ. In expressing the gift of piety, great honor, though never the adoration or worship of latria, is due to members of the Church Triumphant, the Communion of Saints who reside with the Father in Heaven. We can show them this honor by learning about them, each of whom imitated Christ in his or her unique life, that we might learn to do so in the context of our own lives.

We can also show the saints honor by praying to them for their intercession. Our *Catechism* states clearly that the saints who have preceded us into Heaven serve as "a cloud of witnesses"

(Heb. 12:1). Further, "they contemplate God, praise him and constantly care for those whom they have left on earth" (CCC 2683). Scripture reveals that around God's throne in Heaven are "golden bowls full of incense, which are the prayers of the saints" (Rev. 5:8). Those saints experiencing the Beatific Vision of God have no need to pray for themselves. Their prayers are for us, and they welcome our requests that they should offer up their heavenly incense to God for our benefit. In the parable of the talents, Jesus told us that God's faithful servants will be placed in charge over much when they enter into the joy of the Master (Matt. 25:21, 23). The prayers they offer up for us are part of their exalted service, and we should pray to them "to intercede for us and for the whole world" (CCC 2683). We honor them by requesting that they exercise these exalted duties, so to speak, for the sake of our souls and for the souls in Purgatory.

Honoring Others above Ourselves

Let's look again at Paul's words to the Christians in Rome: "Love one another with brotherly affection; outdo one another in showing honor" (Rom. 12:10). We are all called to be saints in the making, and we owe honor and love to even the seemingly least among us. St. Thomas writes about the virtue of *dulia*, "whereby we pay honor and other things pertaining thereto to those who are in a higher position" (*ST*, II-II, q. 103, art. 1). Further, "honor denotes a witnessing to a person's excellence." The kind of honor we give to the saints in Heaven is dulia, whereby we acknowledge their excellence in having finished the race with God's grace, having attained the highest of all positions in Heaven!

The virtue of dulia is not only for the saints in Heaven, though. St. Paul bids us to "outdo one another in showing honor," and

Thomas speaks of this dulia "in a wide sense as denoting any kind of excellence" (*ST*, II-II, q. 103, art. 4). It is in this sense that Paul also bids us, "In humility count others better than yourselves" (Phil. 2:3). This may seem odd, considering our first step toward holiness and Heaven was *truth*. Are others always truly better than we are? Well, St. Augustine has provided an interesting answer to this paradox: "Bethink you that some persons are in some hidden way better than you, although outwardly you are better than they" (as cited in *ST*, II-II, q. 161, art. 6). How often we may be tempted to call to mind our own virtues and good deeds, giving ourselves the benefit of the doubt and providing excuses if we act less than charitably, while presuming the worst about others' behaviors. We might do well to consider all of the good deeds others may have done of which we have no clue! Indeed, how sad if we were to find someday that a person we have dishonored has honored us, though we knew it not. Let's heed the Apostle's advice, then, and get down to business in outdoing others, not in proclaiming our accomplishments but in showing honor to them, realizing that their hidden gifts and virtues may well exceed our own—and thanking God for it!

The Honorability of Modesty

In the Latin Bible Thomas used, Jerome had translated Paul's *semna* as *pudica*. Latin dictionary definitions of *pudica* include "chaste," "pure," and "modest." The English translation I have for Thomas's writings in his commentary on Philippians uses the word *modest*, and Thomas wrote a question with two articles on the *virtue of modesty* (*ST*, II-II, q. 160). Interestingly, in his commentary on Philippians, Thomas cites James to elaborate on Paul's "whatever is modest": "But the wisdom of above is first pure" (James 3:17). Peeking at the original Greek used in this verse from James, we find the word *hagne*, often translated as "pure" or "holy," rather than *semna*.

Well, Paul did indeed advise us to think about whatever is *hagne*, but that will be our subject matter two chapters down the road. One lesson I think we can glean from such words and their various translations hints at the interrelationships between all the virtues, as we will address thoroughly in chapter 7. For now, however, perhaps it will be worthwhile to consider what Thomas wrote in the *Summa* about the virtue of modesty, drawing not from the Latin word *pudica* but from *modestia*, and how it might help us to think about whatever is honorable.

Thomas tells us that the virtue of modesty serves the virtue of *temperance*,[23] which reins in desires most difficult to moderate, "the concupiscible pleasures of touch"—namely, our desires for things such as food, drink, and sensual pleasures. Still, he notes that whenever we find a special virtue about some matter of great importance, we will also find allied virtues that address related matters of less relative importance. For example, the virtue of *magnificence* regulates the outlay of great sums of money for noble works, while the virtue of *liberality* regulates less costly acts of generosity. Thomas follows Cicero, who placed modesty as a virtue related to temperance. In this regard, the virtue of *modesty* reins in pleasures less physically vehement than pleasures of the flesh, especially desires to be noticed and esteemed by others by the way we use, display, and dress our bodies.

[23] Please note that in chapter 7, I will provide tables highlighting the hierarchical arrangement of dozens of virtues serving the cardinal virtues of temperance, fortitude, justice, and prudence.

Thomas also cites Philippians, just a few verses back from our theme verse, in this context: "Let your modesty be known to all men" (Phil. 4:5, D-R).[24] He explains further that we exercise the virtue of modesty in our *outward actions*, which are observable to others and also in terms of the "inner man," the way in which we modestly think about ourselves. In a sense, then, we might think of modesty as a virtue that helps keep us from seeking honor from others for truly honorable traits we may possess and, even more so, from traits not truly worthy of honor at all. We should always strive to do honorable things for their own sakes and not so that we might be honored. This is certainly something worth thinking about in our day, when so many celebrities with so little modesty act and dress in ways that draw attention to themselves and that may inspire their young followers to follow them on their path away from modesty and honor. Rather, true modesty should, as St. Paul advised, help us to keep seeking ways to outdo others in honoring others.

[24] The RSVCE has *forbearance* instead of *modesty*, though *forbearance* itself is synonymous with *moderation* and *self-control*.

Summing Up Step 2: Honor

In this chapter, we took our first step beyond the object of the intellect (truth) to the object of our appetites, desires, and will (honor) in the sense of good that exists in a thing itself, in the highest form in God and in lesser but still honorable form in all the angels and the saints, in every one of us, and, in a sense, in everything God created. We looked at related ideas in St. Thomas's writings on latria and on the virtues of religion, piety, dulia, and modesty, as well as the Holy Spirit's gift of piety, whereby we honor God as our Father and the members of the Communion of Saints as our brothers and sisters. In our next chapter, we will climb to step 3 as we strive to think deeply about "whatever is just," but first, let us give due honor—indeed what is called *hyperdulia*—to the one holy saint most deserving of our honor.

Think about This Saint #2

Blessed Mother Mary

All generations will call me blessed.

—Luke 1:48

Let's recall *latria*, the unique honor we owe to God alone, and *dulia*, the honor—though not worship—we owe to every person, as we set our sights on something in between the two, a person to whom we owe *hyperdulia*: not worship, but a special honor beyond what is owed to all other creatures. Let's start with some insights from St. Thomas Aquinas and his great teacher, St. Albert the Great.

St. Albert notes that when the archangel Gabriel addressed the Virgin Mary as "full of grace" (Luke 1:28), he essentially gave her a new name, a name that no other creature in the universe could claim. St. Thomas explained that Mary was so full of God's grace that, through its superabundance, (1) every possible grace, virtue, and gift of the Holy Spirit filled her soul; (2) grace overflowed from her soul into her body (recall that she would be assumed bodily into Heaven); and (3) "grace overflows from her onto all mankind."[25] This is why we call her the Mediatrix of All Graces and pray for her powerful intercession.

Central to St. Albert's Mariology is her *divine maternity*, her predestined honor to be the bearer of God incarnate, for an even higher grace than being the son of God by adoption (as are all baptized Christians) is to be the Mother of God. Indeed, ever the

25 St. Thomas Aquinas, *The Aquinas Catechism: A Simple Explanation of the Catholic Faith by the Church's Greatest Theologian* (Manchester, NH: Sophia Institute Press, 2000), 165.

logician, like his student Thomas, Albert notes in his book the *Mariale* that to be "the Mother of God by nature though not God" is a mean between "being the Son of God by nature and Truly God, and being the son of God by adoption and not God." The only higher state for Mary would be divinity itself. There, of course, Albert, Thomas, and the Catholic Church never go, knowing full well the essential difference between the created and the Creator, even when considering His most beloved and blessed creature.

So although we would never offer the Blessed Mother the latria or worship due to God only, we are called to offer her *hyperdulia*, the highest form of honor we can give to a human being. God told us to honor our fathers and our mothers. Jesus has given His Mother the highest of all honors: to reside with Him, body and soul, in Heaven, even now before His Second Coming; and surely He rejoices when we show her the highest of honor, when peoples of all generations do indeed called her blessed.

Let's conclude with a beautiful reflection from St. Albert, showing his palpable love and honor for the Blessed Mother, which should inspire us to feel the same:

> Oh, how sweet is Mary's image! See, what care artists take to make it surpass in beauty those of other saints. See how solicitous are the faithful to show it due veneration. Churches are adorned with her pictures that our thoughts may dwell devoutly on her. In heaven we shall behold not her image in marble or on canvas, but her own most beautiful soul and body. We shall gaze on her sweet countenance, and its beauty shall ravish us through eternity.[26]

[26] Cited in St. Albert's College, ed., *St. Albertus Magnus* (Racine, WI: St. Catherine's Press, 1938), 19, from the *Mariale*.

Justice for All

Justice is a habit whereby a man renders to each one his due by a constant and perpetual will.

—St. Thomas Aquinas, *ST*, II-II, q. 58, art. 1

Justice is the crowning glory of the virtues.

—Cicero, *De Officiis* (*On Duties*)

St. Thomas's Thoughts on Philippians 4:8–9

Object of the Intellect (Truth)	***Objects of the Appetite (Good)***	Good beyond What Is Necessary	Motivators of Action	Fruits of the Acts
True	Modest (good in itself)	Lovely (leads to friendship)	Virtue (habits within us)	God: "The God of peace will be with you."
	Just (good directed to neighbor)	Gracious (leads to good reputation)	Praise of discipline (instruction learned from someone else)	
	Holy (good directed to God)		Thinking (internal)	
			Doing (external)	

St. Paul	Latin Vulgate	RSVCE	St. Thomas
dikaia	*justa*	just	just

Doing Justice Justice: Definition, Parts, and Varieties

In the next step up our Pauline spiritual staircase, St. Paul advises us to think about whatever is *dikaia*, which is *justa* in Latin and *just* in English. So just what is *dikaia*, *justa*, or *just*? Let us begin by examining definitions of *justice* from great thinkers, including a great Greek philosopher and two great Latin-writing theologians, all of whom are addressed in the writings of St. Thomas Aquinas (*ST*, II-II, q. 58, "Of Justice"):[27]

- Per St. Isidore of Seville: "Rendering to each one his right is so to be just because he respects the rights of others."
- Per Aristotle, justice is "a habit which makes a man capable of doing what is just, and of being just in action and in intention," and "justice is a habit whereby a man renders to each one his due by a constant and perpetual will."
- Per St. Augustine: "Justice is love serving God alone."

Next, let us see how St. Thomas clarified the meanings of each of these definitions, beginning with St. Isidore's reference to "rights." Indeed, Thomas's first question in his incredibly

[27] Precise citations to texts from Aristotle, Augustine, and Isidore can be found here in the *Summa*.

thorough treatment of justice—a full 66 questions and an astounding 302 articles—begins not with question 58, "Of Justice," but with question 57, "Of Right." He tells us that the word *justice* derives from the Latin word *jus* (or *ius*), which means "right." A fundamental act of rendering each person his "due," in Aristotle's language, is to respect his fundamental rights. And what are fundamental rights? Borrowing from the Greco-Roman and Judeo-Christian heritage of "natural law" and "natural rights," the American Founding Fathers wrote in our Declaration of Independence that all men are created equal and are "endowed by their Creator with certain inalienable Rights, that among these are Life, Liberty, and the Pursuit of Happiness." These are among the most fundamental rights we must render to one another, in man's just laws, mirroring the justice of God's divine law.

One very pithy definition of *justice*, then, is "to render to each person his rightful due." Of course, if St. Thomas could devote 302 articles in more than 250 pages to justice in the *Summa*, we can rightly surmise that there remains a lot more to be said about justice. Let's begin with a look at two more dimensions of the definition of *justice*.

Aristotle's definition mentions justice as a "habit" through which we render each person his or her rightful due, a habit that makes us "capable of doing what is just, and of being just in action and in intention." In addressing this statement in his commentary on Aristotle's *Nicomachean Ethics*, Thomas elaborates that justice is a habit that brings about three effects within us: "The first is an *inclination* to a work of justice in accord with which a man is said to be disposed to just works. The second is a just *action*. The third is that a man *wants* to perform just actions."[28]

[28] Commentary on Aristotle's *Nicomachean Ethics*, 281.

Now, as for the word *habit*, note well that for Aristotle and Thomas (and, in fact, for all of us), *habits are tendencies we build in ourselves* to think, desire, and act in certain ways, good habits being *virtues* and bad habits being *vices*. Virtuous acts flow from virtues as sins flow from vices. Justice, then, as a good habit, is indeed a *virtue* we are called to build in ourselves. As the virtue of justice grows in our souls, we develop a habitual tendency or inclination toward justice rather than injustice, we perform just acts, and indeed, we desire to do so. If we are to heed St. Paul's advice to "think about" justice, we will think about ways we can build this righteous and beautiful habit in our souls.

Of course, as much as St. Paul admired the natural wisdom of ancient philosophers such as Aristotle, he knew well of the one God of Abraham, Isaac, and Jacob and of His holy Son, who had come to earth, suffered, died, and rose again for our salvation. Paul's Christian understanding of justice transcends the merely natural plane and reaches all the way up to God. This we see in St. Augustine's definition of *justice* as "love serving God alone." Indeed, the virtue of justice is served in every one of God's Ten Commandments. When we worship only the true God, when we refrain from using His name in vain, and when we honor Him on the Lord's Day, we render what is due to our Maker. When we honor our parents and abstain from killing, adultery, stealing, false witness, and coveting our neighbor's wife and goods, we render due rights to others. Lest Augustine's reference to serving God "alone" be misunderstood to exclude what is due to others here on earth, Thomas clarifies as follows: "Just as love of God includes love of neighbor … so too the service of God includes rendering to each one his due." As God freely shares His love with us, He bids us share our love with those around us. If you'll forgive my attempt at a rhyme to remember:

"Rendering our neighbors their rightful due is precisely the right and just thing to do."

The Parts of Justice

Our Catholic tradition teaches that virtues have "parts," and we'd be wise to keep as many parts as possible in stock in our souls. Let's take a quick look at the inventory list for the parts that serve justice, before we examine each individual part:

Parts of the Virtue of Justice

Integral Parts	**Subjective Parts**	**Potential Parts**
Doing good	Commutative justice	Religion, piety
Avoiding evil	Distributive justice	Observance, gratitude
		Vengeance, truth
		Friendliness, liberality

A Thomistic Guide to Our Parts Inventory[29]

When St. Thomas addresses justice, as well as the other three cardinal virtues—temperance, fortitude, and prudence—he

[29] Readers of my book *12 Life Lessons from St. Thomas Aquinas* will note that the material in this section is moderately modified from the text of the section titled "On Keeping All the Parts of Justice in Stock" in chapter 12: "Justice Begins at Home."

stresses that each virtue is made complete by three *kinds* of parts:

- *Integral parts.* The first kind, integral parts, are "the conditions the occurrence of which are necessary for virtue" (*ST*, II-II, q. 143). In other words, the integral parts are the "must-haves" of the virtues—as "wall, roof, and foundation" are to a house, as Thomas says. If it is missing any integral part, the cardinal virtue is incomplete and imperfect and cannot be fully expressed.
- *Subjective parts.* The second kind are *subjective* parts, "which are its species; and the species of a virtue have to be differentiated according to difference of matter or object" (*ST*, II-II, q. 143). (We'll flesh this out while addressing the difference between commutative and distributive justice).
- *Potential parts.* Finally, we have *potential* parts, which Thomas also calls secondary or annexed virtues. "The potential parts are the virtues connected with it, which are directed to certain secondary acts or matters, not having, as it were, the whole power of the principal virtue" (*ST*, II-II, q. 48).

Next, let's take a quick parts inventory. The hall of justice, we might say, sits upon the foundation of the *integral parts*, which guide our moral dealings with others, summarized most simply as "Do the good" and "Do not do evil." The law courts of a nation's Department of Justice generally spring into action to investigate possible violations of that second, negative principle. If we do evil to others and deprive them of life, liberty, or property, we must face the penalties prescribed by our community. But the positive aspect of justice is its "principal part," per St. Thomas (*ST*, II-II, q. 79, art. 1). This is the kind of justice pronounced most succinctly and fully by Jesus Christ when He gave us the summary of the commandments: to love God with all that we are and to love our neighbors as ourselves and—the Golden Rule—to "do unto others" as we would have them do unto us. Christ then, intertwines justice with brotherly love as we seek not only not to hurt our brothers and sisters but to actively help them while here on earth and, the good Lord willing, on their way to Heaven.

The *subjective parts* of justice are the two primary "species" or subject matters of justice. *Distributive justice* deals with matters of doing good and avoiding evil that impact entire communities or nations. It is most closely related to the realm of "social justice." The *Catechism* notes that *distributive justice* "regulates what the community owes its citizens in proportion to their contributions and needs (2411). *Commutative justice* "corresponds to the order of one private individual to another" (*ST*, II-II, q. 61, art. 1). Although it is very important to work for a just society, we must remember that justice must always begin and continue at home. In the words of *Catechism*: "Without commutative justice, no other form of justice is possible" (2411). In the powerful words of Jesus Christ:

> How can you say to your brother, "Let me take the speck out of your eye," when there is the log in your own eye? You hypocrite, first take the log out of your own eye, and then you will see clearly to take the speck out of your brother's eye. (Matt. 7:4–5)

Justice must begin in our own hearts—and eyes!

As for the *potential*, *annexed*, or *related* virtues serving justice, they provide an incredibly rich understanding of just how we can "think about," and *practice*, the virtue of justice in our homes, in our churches, and in our societies. Let's take a very terse inventory of these parts before we move on.[30]

Religion, perhaps surprisingly, "falls short" of the full virtue of justice but only because justice involves rendering to another "his rightful due in equal measure" and religion regards what we owe God. Because God, through His boundless generosity, is the very source and sustainer of our existence, we can never give Him back *in equal measure* what He has given us. God, of course, is quite aware of this fact! Religion, Thomas says, is still "the chief of the moral virtues" (*ST*, II-II, q. 81, art. 6), and God expects us to render Him His rightful due only within our limited capacity—through the *virtue of religion*, which comprises *interior* acts, including prayer and devotion, and *exterior* acts, including adoration, sacrifices, tithes, oaths, and vows.

Piety and religion might easily be conflated, and indeed, they should go hand in hand. While religion honors God as our Creator, piety honors God not only as our Creator but also as our *Father*. Further, as we see in God's fourth commandment, piety extends to our earthly parents and to our nation (often referred to as one's fatherland or motherland). St. Thomas has made clear that "man is debtor chiefly to his parents and country after God." If I might borrow words from the Holy Mass, "it is truly right and just" to give God thanks—and to give our parents and our homelands thanks as well.

[30] More-detailed descriptions can be found in my *12 Life Lessons from St. Thomas Aquinas* and *Unearthing Your Ten Talents*. The most detailed descriptions of potential virtues annexed to justice may be found in *ST*, II-II, qq. 81, 101, 102, 103, 104, 106, 108, 109, 114, 117, and 120.

Observance is the virtue by which "we pay worship and honor to those who excel in some way in honor" (*ST*, II-II, q. 102, 2, citing Cicero). This virtue's two main parts are *dulia* and *obedience*. Dulia, as we saw in our last chapter, is honor paid to another person's excellence, giving honor where honor is due. Thomas says that dulia is shown through words and deeds, by gestures such as bowing and saluting, and he reminds us that in every other person we can find some quality or talent that exceeds our own. Therefore, we all owe one another some measure of the respect and honor of dulia. Indeed, our own good St. Paul has made this quite clear: "In humility count others better than yourselves. Let each of you look not only to his own interests, but also to the interests of others" (Phil. 2:3–4). As for the second key component of *obedience*, we are to obey legitimate authority figures placed over us (except, of course, in the hopefully rare cases in which they would command sinful actions). Of course, the greatest authority of all is that of God. Justice and love cannot exist without obedience to God's will. As the beloved apostle had told us: "He who says 'I know him' but disobeys his commandments is a liar, and the truth is not in him; but whoever keeps his word, in him truly love for God is perfected" (1 John 2:4–5).

Gratitude. While religion, piety, and observance render God, our parents and nation, and those excelling us in some way, their rightful due, the virtue of *gratitude* seeks to repay our debts to all who provide any kind of benefit. St. Paul advised: "Give thanks in all circumstances" (1 Thess. 5:18). The Roman Stoic Seneca wrote a wonderful book on gratitude called *De Beneficiis* (*On Benefits*). St. Paul was well versed in Stoic philosophy, and indeed, as we noted before, in the early centuries after Christ, a text circulated purporting to be fourteen letters exchanged between

St. Paul and Seneca, which are now recognized to be spurious. Nonetheless, St. Thomas Aquinas mines extensive insights from Seneca's authentic writings when examining gratitude, citing him more often than even St. Augustine or Aristotle. For just a small sample or two: Seneca wrote, "Do you wish to repay a favor? Receive it graciously"; and even if we are benefited by someone so rich and powerful that we can never repay him in kind, we can still repay by our attitude, our facial expression, our words, and our deeds, as Seneca notes, with "good advice, frequent fellowship, affable and pleasant conversation without flattery." Further, the grateful "outpourings of one's heart" should be heard not only within the earshot of the benefactor but within the hearing of others, thus repaying the benefactor with public honor. And what of the ungrateful? Let's end with some wisdom from Jesus Christ and St. Thomas Aquinas. Jesus told us, "Lend, expecting nothing in return" (Luke 6:35). Quite fittingly, St. Thomas advises that "he that bestows a favor must not at once act the part of a punisher of ingratitude, but rather of a kindly physician, by healing ingratitude with repeated favors" (*ST*, II-II, q. 107, art. 4).

Vengeance (or vindication). It might seem strange to see vengeance (*vindicta* in Latin) as a virtue serving justice, but St. Thomas borrows from Cicero, who tells us that "by vengeance we resist force, or wrong, and in general, what is obscure (i.e., derogatory), either by self-defense or by avenging it." Vengeance, as a virtue, entails developing the habit of punishing wrongdoing within the realm of one's rightful authority and in the spirit of helping the wrongdoer—or at least protecting innocent victims. Per Thomas, "vengeance is lawful and virtuous so far as it tends to the prevention of evil" (*ST*, II-II, q. 108, art. 3). Those with the virtue of vengeance will be slow to take vengeance for wrongdoings they themselves receive, "but they do not bear with them so as to endure the wrongs inflicted on God and their neighbor" (q. 108, art. 1). Vengeance must be exercised with great care, and punishment should be delayed while one is angry so that it won't be excessive and harm the wrongdoer.

Truth, as we noted before, is something we rightfully owe one another. Who wants to be lied to? Further, God has instructed us in the eighth commandment not to bear false witness against our neighbor. What we believe or know should correspond to what we say. To tell the truth is a good act. To develop within ourselves the habit of telling the truth, then, is a moral virtue essential to justice. Of course, we should not forget that prudence is a virtue as well, and though we should not lie, neither should we speak truths with a malicious intent, as in derogatory gossip.

Friendliness. Thomas explains that the friendliness (*amicitia*) that is called affability (*affabilitas*) is part of the virtue of justice and something we rightfully owe to every person we meet. Not everyone can be a close friend, but God crafted us as social beings who derive joy from one another. We should not rob others of that joy by rudeness, neglect, or disrespect. A brief hello or an acknowledging nod and a smile to the person we pass on the street or with whom we share an elevator are among the simplest ways not only to "think about" whatever is just, but to *live* it.

Liberality means freely giving, deriving from the Latin adjective *liber*, "free." As to its relationship to justice, St. Thomas notes that "justice gives what is his, whereas liberality gives another what is one's own" (*ST*, II-II, q. 117, art. 5). Liberality is, in a sense, justice that goes the extra mile, a generosity beyond the call of legal duty and of nature. Thomas captures liberality's essence so well: "To spend money on oneself is an inclination of nature; hence to spend money on others belongs properly to virtue" (*ST*, II-II, q. 117, art. 5). Such liberality does not mean reckless giving, however. Thomas employs an apt military metaphor here, noting that a virtuous soldier's fortitude consists not only of wielding his sword in battle but in sharpening it between battles and storing it in its sheath. So, too, liberality means not only giving away money but always using reasonable means to earn money and save it, so that it can be employed when it is truly needed—to serve the needs of justice and liberality.

So which parts of justice did you find in or out of stock in your soul? The more we can think about justice not merely as the abstract name of a legal department or even the name of a cardinal virtue but as something that we can measure in our own souls by our daily acts toward God and neighbor, the more we will move from *thinking about* justice to *living it.*

More Ways to Think about Justice

Justice is truly a many-splendored thing. A famous condiment maker boasts of "57 varieties" of its products, and although I count only eight main types or varieties of justice in St. Thomas Aquinas's writings, each one can give us something to think about, such as how we can exercise them in our daily lives. We've briefly tasted distributive and communicative justice already; now let's take another taste of them and six other varieties, too, as I lay them out on this table.

Varieties of Justice[31]

Type of Justice	Description
Distributive	Distributive justice is one of two "subjective parts" of justice — that is, what justice is all about. Distributive justice is the relation between a whole and its parts. It refers to the way in which a community distributes common goods to each individual.
Commutative	The other subjective part of justice, commutative justice, regards the relation of one part to another. It refers to private individuals and the mutual dealings between them.
Political	Political justice refers to governmental systems and institutions set up for citizens within a *polis* (community) based on natural rights or on legal agreement or consent between private individuals or by public agreement regarding community goods.
General	General justice refers to the virtue by which a person is a good citizen and acts for the welfare of the common good.
Legal	Legal justice is the expression of general justice in the form of laws designed to benefit the common good.

[31] Distributive and commutative justice are defined in *ST*, II-II, q. 61, art. 1; legal justice in q. 58, art. 6; particular and domestic justice in art. 7; political justice in q. 57, art. 2; and metaphorical justice in q. 58, art. 2. This summary first appeared in my *12 Life Lessons from St. Thomas Aquinas: Timeless Spiritual Wisdom for our Turbulent Times* (Manchester, NH: Sophia Institute Press, 2018), 280–281.

Type of Justice	Description
Particular	Particular justice directs individuals immediately to the good of other individuals.
Domestic	Domestic justice refers to unique, intimate relationships within a household, such as that between husband and wife, or father and son, in which each person is, in a sense, a part of the other.
Metaphorical	Strictly speaking, justice is always social and between persons. Metaphorical justice refers to treating one's principles of action, such as reason and the concupiscible and irascible appetites, as if they were agents of actions themselves. Thus, metaphorically speaking, we can say that in the just person, the appetites obey the commands of reason, rendering reason its rightful due.

God Is Justice (and Mercy)

We saw that justice is truly a many-splendored thing. That is why Cicero called it the "crowning glory of the virtues" and Aristotle said that "justice is more glorious than either the evening or the morning star." Reaching our thought yet higher into the heavens, we must also think about the justice of God Almighty, for indeed, "He made the stars also" (Gen. 1:16). Scripture tells us plainly in Psalm 10:8 [11:7], "The Lord is just, and hath loved justice" (D-R).

St. Thomas Aquinas tells us that God is the just Ruler of the entire universe, fairly distributing a universe of goods. One way God's justice is seen is in the way He gives every creature its rightful due as a creature with its own particular nature—for example, as He gives the powers of growth, nutrition, and reproduction to plants; powers of sensation and movement as well to animals; and powers of intellect and will as well to human beings. In the words of Dionysius, we see that God is truly just "in seeing how he gives to all existing things what is proper to the condition of each and preserves the nature of each one in the order and with the powers that properly belong to it" (as cited in *ST*, I, q. 21, art. 3). We give God our rightful due to the extent that we use our powers for good, as He intended.

We should also think about the fact that while God is supremely *just*, He is extremely *merciful* too. Scripture tells us of God: "[He is] a merciful and gracious Lord" (Ps. 110 [111]:4).

In human terms, there is a connection between *mercy* and *sorrow* based on the Latin word *misericordia*, for "mercy," which means a misery or sadness of the *cor* (heart). The person *feeling* merciful (i.e., experiencing the *passion* of mercy) treats another's misery as if it were his own. The *actions* the merciful person takes to overcome the other person's misery relate to the *effects* of mercy.

Now, God, in His divine essence,[32] does not experience sorrow or misery, but He most certainly takes action to dispel people's misery. Consider that misery can be seen as a defect in a person, in that he lacks the goodness of happiness proper to him. Defects in goodness can be removed only by the perfection of some kind of goodness, "and the primary source is God." Indeed, God bestows perfections not only according to His divine

[32] When God entered time, however, and the Word of God became incarnate, Jesus Christ willingly took on a human nature, through which He could indeed suffer for our sake.

goodness but also according to His *justice*, *liberality*, and *mercy* under different aspects. Let's see how:

- God bestows perfections, *in their absolute sense*, according to His *goodness.*
- God bestows perfections to things *in their proper proportions* according to His *justice.*
- God bestows perfections on things, *not for His own use* but only because of His goodness and His *liberality* (He bestows such things freely and generously).
- God bestows perfections to *remove defects* according to His *mercy.*

Truly, God is good, just, generous, and merciful!

As for people who might think that mercy relaxes and somehow contradicts justice, Thomas states clearly, "God acts mercifully, not indeed by going against his justice, but by doing something more than justice." Suppose a man who owes another man a hundred dollars pays him two hundred instead. That is not an act against justice but an act that adds liberality or mercy. In a similar vein, if we forgive someone who has injured us, it is as though we had given him a gift. Indeed, we have been instructed to do so: "Forgive one another, as Christ has forgiven you" (see Eph. 4:32).

In short, mercy does not contradict or destroy justice but fulfills it. Thus, we read, "Mercy exalteth itself above judgment" (James 2:13, D-R). God is both just and merciful. Would that we would strive to be likewise![33]

[33] Excerpted and adapted from chapter 21 of my book *What Is God?*

Summing Up Step 3: Justice

In thinking about justice, we have considered primarily the good directed toward our neighbor and the many ways we are to express that good as friends, immediate neighbors, family members, fellow citizens, and members of wider groups and communities. We have thought about how justice on earth flows from God's perfect and divine justice, ever in harmony with His liberality and mercy. We might ask ourselves in which particular ways, and with which particular people, we can begin to think and act more justly today.

Think about This Sage #3

Marcus Tullius Cicero (106-43 BC)

For no phase of life, whether public or private, whether one is working on business or in the home, whether one is working on what concerns oneself alone or dealing with another, can be without its moral duty; on the discharge of such duties depends all that is morally right, and on their neglect all that is morally wrong in life.

—Cicero, *De Officiis* (*On Duties*)

Marcus Tullius Cicero, statesman and philosopher, lived before Christ but was one of the greatest pagan champions of justice, republican government, natural law, and natural virtue through his eloquent speeches and treatises, as well as through his deeds. His works have been admired and mined for their ethical wisdom by great Catholic saints and Church Doctors across the millennia.

St. Augustine wrote that Cicero's now lost work *Ad Hortensius*, an exhortation to philosophy dedicated to a man named Hortensius, drew him toward the love of wisdom.

St. Jerome once dreamt he was whipped by angels for being more a Ciceronian than a Christian (though he certainly was not!).

The medieval Cistercian abbot St. Aelred of Rievaulx was so moved by Cicero's essay *De Amicitia* (*On Friendship*) as a young man that in his own beautiful book *Spiritual Friendship* he incorporated more than a third of Cicero's text into his own, though he, like St. Jerome was certainly more Christian than Ciceronian. In Aelred's own words:

> The ideas I had gathered from Cicero's treatise on friendship kept recurring to my mind, and I was astonished that

> they no longer had for me their wonted savor. For now nothing that had not been sweetened by the honey of the most sweet name of Jesus, nothing which had not been seasoned with the salt of Sacred Scripture, drew my affection so entirely to itself.[34]

Nonetheless, St. Aelred started with Cicero's own recipe for friendship and brought it to the heights of culinary perfection with that honey from Jesus and salt from Sacred Writ.

St. Albert the Great held "Tullius" (Cicero) in the highest of regard, agreeing with him that memory, understanding, and foresight are the three parts of the virtue of prudence (to be discussed in more depth in our chapter 7) and recommending Cicero's own method for perfecting the powers of our memory as the best of all.[35]

St. Thomas Aquinas also mined Cicero's writings on justice, government, and the other cardinal virtues time and again in the *Summa Theologica*.[36]

Cicero was a champion of both commutative and distributive justice. His book *On Duties*, for example, addressed to his son, carefully examines what we owe to one another during our private one-on-one interactions. Indeed, through his decisive actions in protecting the republic during what was known as the Cataline Conspiracy, Cicero was, during his lifetime, shown great honor and piety, being declared *Pater Patriae*, "Father of the Country."

[34] Aelred of Rievaulx, *Spiritual Friendship*, trans. Mary Eugenia Laker, S.S.N.D. (Kalamazoo, MI: Cistercian Publications, 1977), 46.

[35] Indeed, this method lies at the heart of my own Catholic books on memory: *Memorize the Faith!*, *Memorize the Reasons!*, *Memorize the Mass!*, *Memorize the Latin Mass!*, *Memorize the Stoics!*.

[36] I direct interested readers to an entire book on the subject: E. K. Rand, *Cicero in the Courtroom of St. Thomas Aquinas* (Milwaukee: Marquette University Press, 1946).

He gave his rightful due and more to his nation during his life and to us today through his writings.

Though he lived before the Word of God became incarnate on earth, Cicero bears some resemblance to later Christian martyrs. After the death of Julius Caesar, he wrote and spoke openly against the tyranny that brought the republic of Rome to its end. On December 7, 43 B.C., Cicero patiently offered his neck when Marc Antony dispatched a solider to bring back for public display in Rome the head that had dared to think and the hands that had dared to write in defense of justice against the reign of tyranny that would come to pass in imperial Rome.

Pure Holiness

Holy, holy, holy is the Lord God Almighty,
who was and is and is to come!

—Revelation 4:8

The word sanctity seems to have two significations. In one way it denotes purity; and this signification fits in with the Greek; for agios (hagios) means unsoiled. In another way it denotes firmness, wherefore in olden times the term sancta was applied to such things as were upheld by law and were not to be violated. Hence a thing is said to be sacred (sancitum) when it is ratified by law.

—*ST*, II-II, q. 81, art. 8

St. Thomas's Thoughts on Philippians 4:8–9

Object of the Intellect (Truth)	***Objects of the Appetite (Good)***	Good beyond What Is Necessary	Motivators of Action	Fruits of the Acts
True	Modest (good in itself)	Lovely (leads to friendship)	Virtue (habits within us)	God: "The God of peace will be with you."
	Just (good directed to neighbor)	Gracious (leads to good reputation)	Praise of discipline (instruction learned from someone else)	
	Holy (good directed to God)		Thinking (internal)	
			Doing (external)	

St. Paul	Latin Vulgate	RSVCE	St. Thomas
hagna	*sancta*	pure	holy

From *Hagna* to *Sancta* to Holy and Pure

St. Paul advised us to think about whatever is *hagna*, translated in the RSVCE as "pure." One good way to begin thinking about it, following St. Thomas Aquinas's lead, is to look at this word's origins and various translations. *Hagios* is the classical Greek word usually translated into English as "sacred" or "holy." We see this in the English word *hagiography*, meaning biographies of holy saints, the English word *saint* itself deriving from the Latin *sancta*, for "sacred" or "holy." We see from our quotation above that Thomas, though using the Latin Vulgate Bible, was well aware of the Greek origin of the word and its two important connotations, meaning "unsoiled" and "inviolable" things upheld by law, as expressed in the Latin word *sanctum* for "a holy or sacred space."

The first connotation, "unsoiled," shows why St. Paul's *hagna* is sometimes translated as "pure." The second connotation, "inviolable," derives from the fact that *hagios* means something that is set apart because it is different or special, as we see in the Holy of Holies, a special sanctuary of the Jewish Temple set aside for God that could be entered only by the high priest on the Day of Atonement. Still, St. Paul would have us think about holiness every day of our lives.

Holiness versus the Virtue of Religion (What Difference Does It Make?)

St. Thomas drills deep into the meaning of *sanctity* or *holiness* in the context of his treatment of the virtue of *religion*, which we met in our last chapter regarding its role as a virtue annexed to justice, specifically addressing *that which we owe to God*. We see from our little table at our chapter's beginning that Thomas described *holiness* as *the good that is directed to God*, so it is a fair enough question to ask how holiness might be the same or different from the virtue of religion. Let's dig deep here ourselves to see just how Thomas thought about this issue.

As is customary in his great *Summa Theologica*, Thomas starts "Whether Religion is the Same as Sanctity" (II-II, q. 81, art. 8) with "objections"—that is, theological arguments that would seem to counter his own reasoned conclusion that religion and holiness (sanctity) are *essentially the same*, though with meaningful logical differences. Let's lay out the top two objections in brief:

1. Some argued that religion is not the same as sanctity, because religion is a *special* virtue with its own unique subject matter of the good involved in doing service to God, while sanctity is a *general* virtue, because it "makes us faithful, and fulfill our just obligations to God," per the writings of the twelfth-century Eastern theologian Andronicus. Hence, sanctity is not the same as religion.
2. Sanctity denotes *purity*. In his *Divine Names*, the theologian Dionysius said that "sanctity is free from all uncleanness, and is perfect and altogether unspotted purity." Purity would seem, then, to correspond to the virtue of *temperance*, which works against bodily

uncleanness. Religion belongs to *justice*, not temperance, so religion and sanctity are not the same.

Thomas begins to rebut these objections by citing from Luke 1:74–75: "That ... we may serve Him ... in holiness and justice." He continues "Now, to serve God belongs to religion [as he had shown earlier in the *Summa* in his first article of II-II, q. 81, on religion]. Therefore, religion is the same as sanctity."

Next, Thomas digs into the etymology we saw in our chapter's opening quotation, revealing how *sanctity*, or *holiness*, implies both an unsoiled *purity* and something considered *inviolable* and ratified by law. He then notes that the Latin word *sanctus* may have its own connection with purity "if it be resolved into *sanguine tinctus*, since, in olden times, those who wished to be purified were sprinkled with the victim's blood," according to St. Isidore's *Etymologies*. (The Latin *sanguis* refers to blood, and *tinctus* means "tinted" or "colored.")

Thomas notes that in either sense (pure or inviolable) *sanctity* is "ascribed to those things that are applied to the divine worship; so that not only men, but also the temple, vessels and such like things are said to be sanctified through being applied to the worship of God." He explains that *purity* is required if we are to raise our minds to God, since "the mind is soiled by contact with inferior things," as silver is debased when it is mixed with lead. So, if we are to unite our minds to the "Supreme Being," we must purify our minds by withdrawing them from lesser things. Consider the lesson of Hebrews 12:14: "Follow peace with all men, and holiness: without which no man will see God" (D-R). Purity of mind is an essential element of the holiness we need if we hope to see God someday in Heaven, in the words of St. Paul, "face to face" (1 Cor. 13:12).

As for the element of *firmness* or *inviolability*, Thomas explains that firmness is required to conform our minds to God because our minds conform to Him as the last end and the first beginning, "and such things must needs be most immovable."[37] This, he says, is why St. Paul said, "I am sure that neither death, nor life . . . shall separate me from the love of God" (see Rom. 8:38–39).[38]

In sum, Thomas concludes as follows:

> Accordingly, it is by sanctity that the human mind applies itself and its acts to God, so that it differs from religion not essentially but only logically. For it takes the name of religion according as it gives God due service in matters pertaining specifically to the Divine worship, such as sacrifices, oblations, and so forth; while it is called sanctity, according as man refers to God not only these, but also the works of other virtues, or according as man by means of certain good works disposes himself to the worship of God.

As for the first of our two main objections, that religion is a *special* virtue and sanctity a *general* virtue, Thomas explains that *in its essence* of being directed toward the worship of God, sanctity or holiness is a *special* virtue and is, in this way, identified with religion. Still, sanctity does possess a kind of *generality*, too, because "it directs the acts of all the virtues to the Divine good, even as legal justice is said to be a general virtue, in so far as it directs the acts of all the virtues to the common good."

As for the second objection that *purity* relates to the virtue of *temperance* while *religion* relates to the virtue of *justice*, Thomas

37 Recall Jesus' declaration: "I am the Alpha and the Omega, the first and the last, the beginning and the end" (Rev. 22:13).

38 Note that both the Latin Vulgate and RSVCE use "us" rather than "me."

notes, "Temperance practices purity, yet not so as to have the character of sanctity unless it be referred to God." We might think of a case in which a person practices sexual purity in a particular instance to avoid public scandal to his reputation rather than to honor God. Thomas concludes this point with a quotation on virginity, from St. Augustine's book *On Virginity*, that "it is honored not for what it is, but for being consecrated to God."

In sum, Thomas concludes that sanctity or holiness differs from the virtue of religion "not really, but logically." It seems that Thomas means that the two differ not in their essence but in how we think about them. St. Paul told us to think about whatever is *hagna* (sanctified, holy, pure), so perhaps if we think about them more carefully, we'll be in a better position to grow holier ourselves and to better offer service to God with all our *mind*—and heart, and soul, and strength (see Mark 12:30).

Purity and Holiness in Our Daily Lives

Thinking seriously about purity and holiness, let's ask ourselves how we might better practice them in our daily lives. Starting with what *not* to do, let's pay close attention to God's warning to the ancient house of Israel: "Her priests have done violence to my law and have profaned my holy things; they have made no distinction between the holy and the common, neither have they taught the difference between the unclean and the clean, and they have disregarded my sabbaths, so that I am profaned among them" (Ezek. 22:26). Are several words that good St. Thomas applied to sanctity ringing any bells in your ears? Notice the reference to violence to God's *law*, to the lack of *distinction* between the *holy* and the *common* and between the *unclean* and the *clean*. Such violations lead to *profanation*, to the defilement and degradation of what is pure and holy. We need to ask ourselves to what extent we render the holy things of God unclean and profane, and we need to remember that the nearest holy things of God to us are our very selves.

St. Paul himself declared: "Do you not know that you are God's temple and that God's Spirit dwells in you? If any one destroys God's temple, God will destroy him. For God's temple is holy, and that temple you are" (1 Cor. 3:16–17). Three chapters later in the same letter, St. Paul returns to the theme: "Do you not know that your body is a temple of the Holy Spirit within you, which you have from God? You are not your own; you were bought with a price. So glorify God in your body" (1 Cor. 6:19–20).

If we are to become holy, we must honor and glorify God through the ways we treat our own bodies because they house His own Holy Spirit. Paul gets us started with advice on how *not* to profane or degrade our bodily temples through sexual sins that denigrate the dignity of those temples. "Shun immorality. Every other sin which a man commits is outside the body; but the immoral man sins against his own body" (1 Cor. 6:18). When St. Thomas addresses *purity* in the context of the virtue of *chastity*, he notes that the two words are used interchangeably at times, as when St. Augustine writes, "Purity is a virtue of the soul" before discussing how purity tempers sexual desires and acts (*ST*, II-II, q. 151, art. 4). In elaborating on *chastity*, Thomas writes, citing Aristotle: "Chastity takes its name from the fact that reason chastises concupiscence, which, like a child, needs, curbing" (*ST*, II-II, q. 151, art. 1). Since the very nature of virtue consists in moderation of things through reason, chastity (or purity), is clearly a human virtue.

Further, while chastity as a special virtue resides in the *soul*, and its primary subject matter is the *body*, there is also a general sense in which chastity relates to spiritual matters. Let's hear Thomas out:

> The word *chastity* is employed in two ways. First, properly; and thus it is a special virtue having a special matter, namely the concupiscences, relating to venereal pleasures. Secondly, the word *chastity* is employed metaphorically; for just as a mingling of bodies conduces to venereal pleasure which is the proper matter of chastity and of lust its contrary vice, so too the spiritual union of the mind with certain things conduces to a pleasure which is the matter of a spiritual chastity metaphorically speaking, as well as of a spiritual fornication likewise metaphorically called. (*ST*, II-II, q. 151, art. 1)

If we are to remain pure and honor all that is holy, we must strive to avoid not only profaning our bodies through sexual sin but profaning our minds from the spiritual sins that flow from focusing on false and worldly idols and diversions, rather than upon God. In describing the vice of spiritual sloth, Thomas lists one sinful "daughter" that flows from it as a mind that wanders after unlawful things, and he cites Aristotle, who wrote: "Those who find no joy in spiritual pleasures have recourse to pleasures of the body" (*ST*, II-II, q. 35, art. 4).[39]

To the contrary, the more we practice bodily and spiritual purity as we strive to distinguish between things profane and things divine, the closer we will grow toward union with God. And one day, should St. Paul's steps lead us all the way to Heaven, we will join in with the chorus of saints and angels singing "Holy, holy, holy is the Lord God Almighty, who was and is and is to come!"

[39] Citing *Nicomachean Ethics*, bk. 10, chap. 6.

Summing Up Step 4: Holiness

Congratulations! You are halfway up St. Paul's staircase. We've thought about the object of the intellect, which is *truth*; the object of the appetite, good in itself, which is *honor*; the good directed to neighbor, which is *justice*; and now, the good directed to God, which is *holiness*. As we continue to ponder holiness in the days and years ahead, how might we strive to make ourselves pure in body and in mind? How might we clearly demarcate the distinction between what is profane and what is holy? Might we set up in our homes a special holy space, with a crucifix, a Bible, and holy art and other sacramentals? Might we act with the utmost respect and reverence every time we step into a church? Might we cast out the profane from our minds—and our tongues—by banishing profanity from our vocabulary, for the greater glory of God? Might we glorify our bodies, the very temples of the Holy Spirit, by striving to keep them pure, not only from sexual sins but from the kinds of man-made foodstuffs and drugs that can profane our bodily temples? What else might we do so that our hearts and minds will be raised as high as they can be toward God while on earth—before, the good Lord willing, we see His holy face in Heaven? These are but a few of many things to think about, and do, as we strive to grow in holiness.

Think about This Saint #4

St. Agnes of Rome (291-304)

To us, also, your servants, who, though sinners, hope in your abundant mercies, graciously grant some share and fellowship with your holy Apostles and Martyrs: with John the Baptist, Stephen, Matthias, Barnabas, Ignatius, Alexander, Marcellinus, Peter, Felicity, Perpetua, Agatha, Lucy, Agnes, Cecilia, Anastasia, and all your saints; admit us, we beseech you, into their company, not weighing our merits, but granting us your pardon, through Christ our Lord.

—Commemoration of the Dead in the Roman Canon

All saints are *hagios* (saintly, holy), as St. Paul bids us to think about. St. Agnes is truly a remarkable saint, being one of seven women mentioned in the ancient Roman Canon (Eucharistic Prayer) of the Mass, and yet I've chosen St. Agnes for our essay on purity and holiness partly for personal reasons—my own and St. Thomas Aquinas's!

You see, I was baptized at St. Agnes Church, belonged to St. Agnes Parish, and attended St. Agnes Elementary School, so she was among the first saints I had ever heard about. I would discover decades later that St. Thomas Aquinas, the man whose writings helped bring me back to Christ, had a special devotion to St. Agnes too. Thomas's friend Br. Reginald of Piperno reported that Thomas carried a relic of St. Agnes upon his chest. One day in 1272, when Reginald fell ill during a journey, Thomas pulled out the relic and prayed for the saint's intercession. When Reginald was cured, Thomas declared that he would provide a special dinner every year for his students on St. Anges's feast day, January 21. Within two years of Reginald's cure, Thomas himself would join his beloved St. Agnes in Heaven.

Why might Thomas have felt such a special devotion to Agnes? Well, Thomas wrote that while every saint in Heaven receives an *aurea*, a spiritual crown, some saints receives additional *aureoles*, or small crowns, for special spiritual triumphs. He wrote that "some special reward is due to virginity, and this is called the aureole" (*ST*, Supp., q. 96, art. 5). We know that "the desires of the flesh are against the Spirit" (Gal. 5:17), so a special crown is due for the spiritual victory of virginity. St. Agnes was such a pure and holy virgin. Born to a wealth family and known for her physical beauty, Agnes, as a young girl, chose to remain a virgin, declaring that Jesus Christ alone would be her spouse.

Thomas writes that aureoles are also reserved for another class of great saints, the holy martyrs, for their most perfect spiritual victories over violent assaults to the body. When St. Agnes declined the marriage proposals of suitors, she was exposed to the Roman authorities as a Christian. To be a Christian was against the law at that time. Constantine, the first Christian emperor, would declare Christianity legal nine years after her death. Refusing to deny Christ, Agnes was eventually sentenced to death and earned that second glowing heavenly crown.

St. Agnes is usually depicted holding a lamb, since the lamb is a symbol of Christ and of holy purity and because the Latin word for "lamb," *agnus*—as in the Agnus Dei (Lamb of God), which we pray at Mass—is so similar to her name. She died on January 21, 303, at the young age of twelve or thirteen.

May this beautiful holy girl with the two small crowns inspire us, as she did St. Thomas, to strive to live pure, holy lives. St. Agnes, pray for us!

Loving Loveliness

It behooves man to be maintained in a becoming order towards other men as regards their mutual relations with each other, in point of both deeds and words, so that they behave towards one another in a becoming manner. Hence the need of a special virtue that maintains the becomingness of this order: and this virtue is called friendliness.

—St. Thomas Aquinas, *ST*, II-II, q. 114, art. 1

Behold, you are beautiful, my love; behold, you are beautiful; your eyes are doves. Behold, you are beautiful, my beloved, truly lovely.

—Song of Solomon 1:15–16

St. Thomas's Thoughts on Philippians 4:8–9

Object of the Intellect (Truth)	**Objects of the Appetite (Good)**	***Good beyond What Is Necessary***	**Motivators of Action**	**Fruits of the Acts**
True	Modest (good in itself)	***Lovely (leads to friendship)***	Virtue (habits within us)	God: "The God of peace will be with you."
	Just (good directed to neighbor)	Gracious (leads to good reputation)	Praise of discipline (instruction learned from someone else)	
	Holy (good directed to God)		Thinking (internal)	
			Doing (external)	

St. Paul	**Latin Vulgate**	**RSVCE**	**St. Thomas**
prosphile	*amabilia*	lovely	lovely

From Loveliness to Friendliness

Now St. Paul bids us think about whatever is *prosphile*–whatever that means! Of course, it is my job to try to explain it. Well, this appears to be the only time this Greek word appears in the New Testament, so we'd better strive to get it right. Per Langenscheidt's *Pocket Dictionary of Classical Greek*, the word means "dear, beloved; pleasing; kind, friendly." In the Latin Vulgate it is rendered *amabilia* (from which we derive *amiable*), and it is rendered "lovely" in the English translation of St. Thomas and in the RSVCE. Now, since *amiable* means "pleasant and friendly" in English, it makes sense that Thomas described it as something that leads to friendship, since we are drawn toward those who are, to quote Langenscheidt once more, "dear, beloved; pleasing; kind, friendly."

The very perceptive and retentive might recall from chapter 3 that St. Thomas enumerated the friendliness (*amicitia*) that is called affability (*affabilitas*) under the virtues that support justice. Although we have the time and energy to form deep, intimate, ongoing friendships with only a relatively few people, we rightfully owe kindness and friendliness to every single person we meet.

I find it quite telling that Thomas classifies what is lovely under "good beyond what is necessary" and notes that it "leads to friendship." Thomas, the man who "baptized" Aristotle, as some say, harvesting the fruits of the truths of his reason for the nourishment of Christ's Church, as we've seen, wrote a commentary on every line of Aristotle's *Nicomachean Ethics*. Aristotle addresses friendship in book 8 of that work, having devoted the first seven books to various moral and intellectual virtues.[40] Thomas comments that, at this point, "he now turns his attention to friendship which is founded upon virtue as an effect of it."[41] Virtue leads to friendship because we are naturally drawn to the goodness of virtue in others, and those of us who acquire virtue will seek to share its fruits with others.

A lovely friendliness is, in a sense, "good beyond what is necessary," for while we are to *honor* things good in themselves and, in *justice*, to render others the good they are due and to direct ourselves in *holiness* toward the good of God, *affability* can be seen as an overflow of sorts, wherein we seek to share freely all forms of goodness with others. Indeed, this desire to share our joy should be visible in our faces, in our eyes, and in our smiles. We appear friendly and beloved to others when we look them in the eye, showing them that we recognize that they are worthy of our attention. Jesus told us that "the eye is the lamp of the body" and "if your eye is sound, your whole body will be full of light" (Matt. 6:22).

St. Thomas explains that "we do not treat strangers with the same intimacy as those who are united to us by special friendship,"[42] and yet "every man is naturally every man's friend

[40] Stay tuned for a full discussion of these classes of virtue in chapter 7.

[41] *Commentary on Aristotle's* Nicomachean Ethics, 476.

[42] Quotations in this section are from *ST*, II-II, q. 114: "Of the Friendliness Which Is Called Affability."

by a certain general love." He cites Ecclesiasticus 13:19: "Every beast loveth its like" (D-R)[43] and explains that this love is shown by outward signs of friendship, "by words or deeds, even to those who are strangers or unknown to us."

Therefore, when we "think about" loveliness, as St. Paul advises, we would do well to think seriously about how we strive to become dear, kind, pleasing, and beloved to our neighbors, by the love and benevolence we express, by the warm acknowledgment of others' presence in our eyes, the welcoming words that issue from our lips, and the gestures that issue forth from our hands and arms—be it a wave, a salute, a handshake, or a hug, as appropriate to particular circumstances. Can we imagine how Jesus, in the flesh, might look at us, acknowledge us, speak to us, and encourage us? Can we remember that Christ is in our neighbor and that we are to be as Christ to him or her?

From Friendliness to Friendship

While friendliness is owed to every man or woman we meet,[44] both St. Paul and St. Thomas wax eloquently on the highest

[43] In the RSVCE, this is Sirach 13:15: "Every creature loves its like, and every person his neighbor."

[44] Thomas does, however, describe some special, limited circumstances in which we should withhold friendly gestures toward others. He starts by citing our own St. Paul (2 Cor. 7:8, D-R): "Although I made you sorrowful by my epistle, I do not repent," and further on (v. 9): "I am glad; not because you were made sorrowful, but because you were made sorrowful unto penance." Thomas adds: "For this reason we should not show a cheerful face to those who are given to sin, in order that we may please them, lest we seem to consent to their sin, and in a way encourage them to sin further."

forms of friendliness: friendship, loveliness, and love itself. Per St. Paul: "So faith, hope, love abide, these three; but the greatest of these is love" (1 Cor. 13:13). Per St. Thomas, "charity is the friendship of man with God," and further, "the principal act of charity is to love" (*ST*, II-II, q. 23. art. 1; q. 27. art. 1). Indeed, Thomas starts his massive treatise on the virtue of *caritas* (charity or love) by demonstrating how *charity is really a state of friendship between man and God*, citing a verse from Paul: "God is faithful, by whom you were called into the fellowship of his Son" (1 Cor. 1:9). Of course, Jesus Himself said, "No longer do I call you servants . . . but I have called you friends" (John 15:15). Further, He declared: "Greater love has no man than this, that a man lay down his life for his friends" (John 15:13)—and then He did just that for us.

Thomas explains, expanding on insights from Aristotle, that in true friendship, we love the friend as we love ourselves; we love him for his own sake and not merely for the fact that he is useful or provides us with pleasure. We rejoice in our friend's existence, we want to be with him, and we wish the best for him and for those dear to him. Not only do we wish him well—we take actions for his benefit to express that love. Indeed, "the love of our neighbor requires not only should we be our neighbor's well-wishers, but also his well-doers" (*ST*, II-II, q. 32, art. 5).[45]

How astounding an honor that the Creator of the universe has extended His deepest friendship to each of us. Indeed, not only does God's friendship express His joy *that* we exist; it *causes* us to exist! Now, how is that for something lovely and friendly without measure!

[45] Cf. 1 John 3:18: "Little children, let us not love in word or speech but in deed and in truth."

Further, God commands us to show our love for Him by loving our neighbor and even ourselves as well, in body and in soul. Thomas compares this love to the heat of a powerful furnace, noting that its heat should extend even to our enemies but that those closest to the furnace should receive the most heat (*ST*, II-II, q. 27, art. 7). This reflects that call to friendliness we owe to all men and women, as well as the special intimate blessing of friendship we share with a relative few friends and relatives.

The Lovely and the Beautiful

We also speak of *lovely* things as being *beautiful*. Indeed, the online *Merriam-Webster Dictionary* defines *lovely* as "(1) delightful for beauty, harmony, or grace: attractive; (2) grand, swell; (3) eliciting love by moral or ideal worth." There is a special kind of loveliness, a special sense of beauty, that attracts a couple to each other, to the sacrament of Matrimony, and to a new generation of life that springs forth from their mutual love.

We started this chapter by quoting the Song of Solomon (1:15–16): "Behold, you are beautiful, my love; behold, you are beautiful; your eyes are doves. Behold, you are beautiful, my beloved, truly lovely." The Song of Solomon is full of praise for physical beauty that represents spiritual beauty as well. This beautiful song of the Old Testament expresses the deep love of a man for his beloved and symbolizes the love between God and His people.

How interesting and fitting that in the last hours of his life, St. Thomas Aquinas, deathly ill and bedridden in the Monastery of Fossanova, in Italy, was asked by the Cistercian monks to explain to them the Song of Solomon.[46] The humble Thomas

[46] Also known as the Song of Songs and the Canticle of Canticles.

demurred, saying, "Give me the spirit of Bernard, and I will present to you an exposition that expresses his spirit," for St. Bernard of Clairvaux, perhaps the greatest of the Cistercians, had written beautifully about that book.

Still, the monks continued to press him, and the Angelic Doctor began his exegesis. Unfortunately, no transcription survives to our knowledge, but Thomas proceeded to provide his commentary until he arrived at the sixth chapter. After reading this verse: "Come, my beloved, let us go forth into the fields" (Song 7:11), Thomas breathed his last breath and joined his beloved Christ in the fields of Heaven. Thomas's dear friend Reginald of Piperno would declare how fitting it was that Thomas would "finish his teaching with the Song of love between Jesus Christ and the faithful soul."[47] Quite lovely, no?

[47] "St. Thomas' Last Days," Thomistica, Sacra Doctrina Project, https://thomistica.net/st-thomas-last-days.

Summing Up Step 5: Loveliness

At our fifth step up St. Paul's staircase, we have taken our first step beyond "the good that is necessary," in St. Thomas's language. We have begun to experience the joy of thinking about what is lovely and about how we can share this joy and loveliness with others. Have we thought much about the utter, infinite loveliness of God Himself? Let's think about this to sum things up. Again, per St. Thomas:

> He produced many and diverse creatures, that what was wanting to one in the representation of divine goodness might be supplied by another. For goodness, which in God is simple and uniform, in creatures is manifold and divided; and hence the whole universe together participates in the divine goodness more perfectly, and represents it better than any simple creature. (*ST*, I, q. 47, art. 1)

Let's think about it from the perspective of loveliness. What do you find lovely? A baby's smile? A loving couple's shared laughter? The warm embrace of long-lost friends who chance upon each other? Some simple act of kindness from a stranger? God, in Himself, is the perfect source from which every form of good or loveliness derives and mirrors Him in its own small ways. Let us think of ways we can mirror God's loveliness, His friendliness, and the fire of His love to everyone we call our neighbor and, even more so, to everyone we call our friend.

Think about This Saint #5

St. Brigid of Kildare (ca. 453-525)

I would like a great lake of ale for the King of the kings.
I should like the family of heaven to be
drinking it through time eternal. . . .
I should like vessels of charity for distribution.
I should like caves of mercy for their company.
I should like cheerfulness to be in their drinking;
I should like Jesus, too, to be there among them.
I should like the three Marys of illustrious renown;
I should like the people of Heaven there from all parts.
I should like that I should be a rent-payer to the Lord;
That, should I suffer distress, He would
bestow upon me a good blessing.

—Ancient Prayer attributed to St. Brigid

Brigid of Kildare, Ireland, is a most affable ancient saint and the subject of countless stories and legends. A patron saint of Ireland, along with Sts. Patrick and Columba, she was so well respected and loved that she was known as "the Mary of the Irish."[48] Though the prayer above has been tracked back only to the eleventh century, whereas Brigid lived in the fifth and sixth, whether she wrote it or not, it surely captures the essence of her lovely and loving personality. Just imagine such heavenly festivities!

Brigid was known and loved for her compassionate acts of mercy for the sick and the poor, along with unmatched sweetness, kindness, and liberal hospitality. A legend relates that it was

[48] For example, in the ancient *Beatha Bhrigidi* (The life of Brigid).

prophesied that St. Brigid would be born neither outside nor inside and that she would bring great good to the world. As the story goes, she was born while her mother, carrying a pail of milk, was crossing the threshold into her house, neither completely outside nor inside! The story may also carry a deeper significance. Brigid's father was a powerful Irish chieftain, and her mother was his unmarried slave. Some argue that part of Brigid's success was due to the fact that she could relate to those of both worlds, both the rich and the poor, the powerful and the oppressed, and she strove mightily to share her love and Christ's gospel with both.

Many stories about Brigid's boundless liberality, or generosity, to man and to beast (as my Irish ancestors are so fond of telling) are rather amusing. She was always giving things away. According to one story, while Brigid was preparing a meal for five guests of the house, a favorite dog stared at her with doleful, hungry eyes. Brigid was cooking up bacon, having been given one large piece for each guest. Her heart went out to the dog, and her hand went out, too, with a nice piece of bacon. And after that, another one. Someone had seen what she had done, and when tempers were starting to flare, her father, Dubhthach, asked her if all of the pieces were still there. She asked him to count them, and to their amazement, five juicy pieces remained in the pan!

Brigid's giving ways did not abate. The poor and the needy were always around, and she could never turn them down; she gave away food or whatever articles were at her disposal within the household. Her father was not at all pleased, and he once arranged to sell her as a servant to his overlord, Dunlang MacEnda, the king of the Province of Leinster. Brigid, though, was always Brigid. While waiting outside in her father's chariot during his negotiations with the king, a leper happened by. Brigid pitied him in his deformity and want, and when he begged for her charity, her heart sank at having nothing to give him, until she spied her father's cherished prize sword which was gilded at the hilt. It remained in the chariot since no one could come armed for an audience with the king. In fact, the sword had been a gift from King Dunlang himself. Brigid bestowed it on the poor leper, and as you might surmise, her father became enraged. Her dragged her before the king, who asked Brigid if she would give away his wealth and possessions too. She answered with honesty that she'd give away all of the wealth of Leinster to the poor, if it were at her disposal. Now, King Dunlang was a Christian, having been baptized by St. Patrick himself, and upon hearing this story and Brigid's reply, he declared that this holy slave girl's status was higher in God's eyes than was theirs. He gave her father a great sword with an ivory hilt, finer than the one that Brigid had given away, and she returned home with her father.

Brigid would go on to establish Ireland's first order of religious sisters, "holy virgins" for Christ, and would travel around in a chariot of her own, spreading good cheer, hospitality, mercy, mirth, and Christ's gospel all about the Emerald Isle for the rest of her life. St. Brigid's feast day is February 1.

St. Brigid, pray for us, that our souls might become as lovely and loving as yours.

Gratitude for Grace

Have regard for your name, since it will remain for you longer than a thousand great stores of gold. The days of a good life are numbered, but a good name endures for ever.

—Sirach 41:12–13

We must now consider the exterior principle of human acts, i.e., God, in so far as, through grace, we are helped by Him to do right; and first we must consider the grace of God; secondly, its cause; thirdly, its effects.

—*ST*, I-II, q. 109, prologue

St. Thomas's Thoughts on Philippians 4:8–9

Object of the Intellect (Truth)	Objects of the Appetite (Good)	***Good beyond What Is Necessary***	Motivators of Action	Fruits of the Acts
True	Modest (good in itself)	Lovely (leads to friendship)	Virtue (habits within us)	God: "The God of peace will be with you."
	Just (good directed to neighbor)	***Gracious (leads to good reputation)***	Praise of discipline (instruction learned from someone else)	
	Holy (good directed to God)		Thinking (internal)	
			Doing (external)	

St. Paul	Latin Vulgate	RSVCE	St. Thomas
euphema	*bonae famae*	gracious	of good fame

From Good Fame to Grace

At the next step up our spiritual staircase, St. Paul bids us to think about whatever is *euphema*, which derives from the Greek words *eu*, "good," and *pheme*, "a saying or report." The Latin Vulgate and St. Thomas Aquinas use the words *bonae famae*, which is why Thomas's English translation is rendered "of good fame." Various English Bible translations use words including *admirable*, *of value*, *commendable*, *of good report*, and *of good repute*. The RSVCE uses the word *gracious*, which provides fodder for yet deeper things to think about, things that St. Paul, St. Thomas, and, without a doubt, St. Augustine ("the Doctor of Grace") would highly recommend! And I think we will find as we go along that nothing leads to *good fame* among Christians like the *grace* that leads to graciousness. Let's begin.

A few years ago, when asked to write an essay about the meaning of life for a secular website, I included this statement: "And if, when our life on this earth has ended, even one person can think of us, smile, and be thankful we were here, that is all for the better."[49] As I think back on that thought now, it may encapsulate

[49] "Dr. Kevin Vost: The Meaning of Life ... and the Virtuous Keys," Excellence Reporter, May 9, 2018, https://excellence

just a little bit of what St. Paul meant by thinking about (and living out) whatever is *euphema*. If we can live in such a way that people who survive us will think about us and have good things to say, for perhaps even the simplest ways we lived out our lives in the service of others and of God, then we have heeded St. Paul's advice.

But let's think a little deeper still. Do those of us among the Church Militant, alive on earth today, have a special title of honor for people of the very highest repute? Indeed, we do, and we all know the title *Saint* for members of the Church Triumphant, in Heaven. To paraphrase Joshua Ben Sirach, these are the people whose good names endure forever. St. Paul encourages us all to honor the saints in Heaven and to live as the saints in our time upon earth. Wonderful! But how can we do it?

Now, this same Paul has declared, just a few verses down from the theme verse for this book, "I can do all things in him who strengthens me" (Phil. 4:13). It is Jesus Christ who gives Paul, and all of us, the strength to lead admirable lives of good repute that will lead us to Heaven. A very important word for God-given strengths of all sorts is *grace*. Thankfully, St. Thomas has graced us with wonderful expositions of God's many generous graces, so let's turn our attention to them next.

Grace Is Essential to Happiness, Holiness, and Heaven

If we grit our teeth and steel our limbs, might we climb St. Paul's staircase on our own power, pulling ourselves by our own bootstraps up through the gates of Heaven? Jesus Himself has told us that the answer is no!

---

reporter.com/2018/05/09/dr-kevin-vost-the-meaning-of-life-and-the-virtuous-keys/.

> Abide in me, and I in you. As the branch cannot bear fruit by itself, unless it abides in the vine, neither can you, unless you abide in me. I am the vine, you are the branches. He who abides in me, and I in him, he it is that bears much fruit, for apart from me you can do nothing. (John 15:4–5)

We gain our spiritual strength and efficacy through the gracious generosity of the power of God Almighty. The idea that we could fulfill God's commandments and merit eternal happiness through the proper use of our own free will and natural powers was at the heart of the fifth-century Pelagian heresy. Pelagius denied the Fall and Original Sin, and his errors were soundly refuted by his contemporary St. Augustine. Thomas tells us that despite our capacities to acquire natural virtue, the attainment of eternal happiness with God is a *supernatural* end, above any natural capacity, especially in our fallen state, with our disordered appetites and will that incline us toward sin.

But God has gladly come to our rescue to open the gates of Heaven to us. In one of his simple, beautiful Lenten reflections on the "Feast of the Holy Lance and the Nails of the Lord" (Friday after the First Sunday of Lent), Thomas cites John 19:34: "One of the soldiers with a spear opened His side, and immediately there came out blood and water" (D-R).[50] He goes on to explain that the Gospel deliberately says "opened" and not "wounded"[51] because through Our Lord's side there was opened to us the gate of eternal life. Then he cites Revelation 4:1: "After these things I looked, and

[50] St. Thomas Aquinas, *Aquinas' Lenten Meditations: 40 Days with the Angelic Doctor*, trans. Fr. Philip Hughes (Manchester, NH: Sophia Institute Press, 2023), 45.

[51] "Pierced" in the RSVCE.

behold a gate was opened to heaven" (D-R). Christ's death for us conquered sin and death, opening for us the gateway to Heaven.

Thomas writes elsewhere, that "the Church is said to be built up with the sacraments *which flowed from the side of Christ while hanging on the Cross*" (*ST*, III, q. 64, art. 3). The Church's *sacraments* are the principal means through which we receive the supernatural *graces* that open the gates to Heaven. Let's take a brief look at the many-splendored things that are God's graces.

Six Kinds of Grace That Lead Us (and Others) to Heaven

1. *Sanctifying grace* is a gift from God that not only perfects the various *powers* of the soul, as the natural virtues do, but also permeates and transforms the very *essence* or nature of the human soul, from which the powers flow. Even the God-infused supernatural virtues of faith, hope, and charity derive from grace, their supernatural source. "For as the acquired virtues enable a man to walk in accordance with the natural light of reason, so do the infused virtues enable a man to walk as befits the light of grace" (*ST*, I-II, q. 119, art. 3). In terms of a pithy definition, sanctifying grace is grace given by God to a person to make him holy and to unite him to God as a participant in the divine nature.
2. *Gratuitous grace* is grace given by God to a person to enable him to help lead *others* toward union with God. Thomas elaborates that Paul rightly further "divides" the gratuitous graces into wisdom, knowledge, miracles, prophecy, discernment of spirits, tongues, and interpretation of speeches (1 Cor. 12:8–10). By use

of these special graces, their receivers display speech and deeds that God alone could produce, thereby teaching and persuading their hearers and witnesses to turn their hearts to God. Lest we despair if we do not display these graces, we should remember Paul's words, noting that not everyone will receive them, for the Holy Spirit "apportions [them] to each one individually as he wills" (1 Cor. 12:11).

3. *Operating grace* is grace that *directly moves us* to will and act, in which our minds are moved, but our minds themselves do not move (as when God gives us the grace to will good instead of evil).
4. *Cooperating grace* is the grace that *strengthens our will* and *gives us the capacity* to do "meritorious works, which spring from the free will"—thus making us ready to receive operating grace and to put it to good use" (*ST*, I-II, q. 111, art. 3).
5. *Prevenient grace* is grace that *precedes* and *causes* a state or act of the soul.
6. *Subsequent grace* is the grace that *follows* as an effect of a prior *effect* of grace. Thomas lists five effects of grace as follows: (1) it heals the soul; (2) it helps us desire the good; (3) it helps us carry out acts to attain the good; (4) it helps us persevere in striving for the good; and (5) it helps our souls reach glory with God. Each of these effects acts as a *cause* (prevenient grace) to the effect (subsequent grace) that follows. Thomas notes, too, that "although the effects of grace may be infinite in number, even as human acts are infinite, nevertheless ... all coincide in this—that one precedes another" (*ST*, I-II, q. 11, art. 4).

Grace is indeed a most amazing thing! And yet, as we will now see, it is far more amazing still. The gift of grace is caused by God alone, and it surpasses the power of any created nature, even that of the angels, "since it is nothing short of a partaking of the Divine Nature, which exceeds every other nature." Indeed, Thomas says that, through grace, "God alone should deify, bestowing a partaking of the Divine Nature by a participated likeness" (*ST*, I-II, q. 112, art. 1). Through His grace, God, in a sense, *defies us* and makes us like Him to a limited extent, within our capacities as creatures. We need to do our part to prepare our hearts for God's grace by turning our free will toward Him. And yet God alone is ultimately the cause and mover even of our free will. Grace, then, is truly and wholly a wondrous gift from God, and whoever has received it with open arms, heart, and soul will become "of good repute" from anyone who loves God.

Staircase or Elevator?

So then, if it is truly God's grace that raises us to Heaven (which it is!), should we imagine we are climbing Paul's staircase to Heaven—or riding Thérèse's elevator all the way to the top? Is there really any sense in which we earn or "merit" our heavenly reward? Let's see what good St. Thomas has to say.

In a sense, Thomas says we can merit our heavenly reward. He starts by citing the prophet Jeremiah: "It is written (Jer. 31:16) 'There is a reward for thy work.' Now a reward means something bestowed by reason of merit. Hence it would seem that a man may merit from God" (*ST*, I-II, q. 114, art. 2). Although we cannot lay claim as a right to anything from God, since we are in no way His equal, and all of man's natural good comes from God in the first place, God, nonetheless, has helped us achieve the merit that we could not achieve on our own. As a modern commentator on the *Summa* aptly explains: "The basis of this blessed situation lies in the fact that human free will, although moved by supernatural grace, actually does cooperate with God's will in accepting and using grace."[52] So then, we can merit even our heavenly reward, but only with the help of God's *grace*.

God's graces were first opened to us through the sacrament of Baptism, and they are strengthened at Confirmation. Graces flow from all seven sacraments. Still, if we should turn away from God after receiving His grace and fall into mortal sin, we cannot merit for ourselves a restoration of God's grace after our fall; our restoration itself must be a work of God's grace. The sacrament of Reconciliation will restore God's grace to us.

While in a state of grace, Thomas tells us, we may merit an *increase* of grace or charity. He cites Proverbs 4:18 (D-R): "But the path of the just as a shining light, goeth forward and increaseth even to perfect day, which is the day of glory." Thomas notes that every meritorious act causes an increase of grace, and the last end of grace is eternal life. "But just as eternal life is not given at once, but in its own time, so neither is grace increased at once, but in its own time, viz., when a man is sufficiently disposed for the increase of grace" (*ST*, I-II, q. 114, art. 8).

52 Msgr. Paul J. Glenn, *A Tour of the Summa* (Rockford, IL: TAN Books, 1978), 183.

Summing Up Step 6 (or Perhaps the Sixth Floor): Graciousness

Let's go back to our staircase, or elevator, if you prefer. It seems that both are apt metaphors. God's grace supplies the strength to lift us to Heaven, but we must be willing to cooperate and do our own part, be it making the effort to ascend the next step or pushing the right elevator button and not hopping out before we hit the top floor! Next stop, stair (or floor) 7.

Think about This Saint #6

St. Joseph

An angel of the Lord appeared to him in a dream, saying, "Joseph, son of David, do not fear to take Mary your wife, for that which is conceived in her is of the Holy Spirit; she will bear a son, and you shall call his name Jesus, for he will save his people from their sins."

—Matthew 1:20–22

As we begin to think of St. Joseph as a model of a man "of good repute" who willingly accepted and ran with God's graces, let's recall again the words of Sirach that started our chapter: "Have regard for your name, since it will remain for you longer than a thousand great stores of gold. The days of a good life are numbered, but a good name endures for ever" (41:12–13). The name of Joseph, foster father of Our Lord Jesus Christ, has indeed endured with honor for more than two thousand years now.

Moving now to some wisdom from the New Testament, let's recall a few words from Jesus' beloved disciple: "Let us not love in word or speech but in deed and in truth" (1 John 3:18). What a powerful example we find in St. Joseph, for he is honored around the world and in Heaven as the patron saint of the universal Church and of families as well, though Scripture does not record a single *word* he said. He is known to us by his *deeds*, and keeping in mind this chapter's theme, about how God's supernatural grace perfects our souls by exceeding human nature, consider how we first meet Joseph in Matthew's Gospel.

Joseph has learned that Mary, his betrothed, is with child "before they came together ... and her husband Joseph, being a just man and unwilling to put her to shame, resolved to send her away quietly" (Matt. 1:18–19). Joseph knew the natural laws of biology, but he was not angry with Mary, for he knew the natural law of virtue and justice as well, and he was unwilling to expose Mary to shame. Yet, as we learn in the verse that begins our essay, Joseph was graced through God by the presence of an angel, who appeared to him in a dream and explained that Mary bore the child of no man but of the Holy Spirit. Matthew tells us: "All this took place to fulfill what the Lord had spoken by the prophet: 'Behold, a virgin shall conceive and bear a son, and his name shall be called Emmanuel' (which means, God with us)" (Matt. 1:22–23). Upon awakening, Jospeh did precisely what the angel told him and took Mary for his wife.

Again, we have not a single quotable quote from Joseph in Scripture, and Scripture is silent on when he died on earth and was born in Heaven. Nonetheless, he is held in the highest regard for how he accepted God's command, loved the woman so full of God's grace, and raised the very Word and Son of God, who willingly became small as He become the fruit of Mary's womb in taking on a human nature so that He would conquer sin and death for us.

We know through Joseph's actions that he became the model loving husband and father, doing whatever was required to protect and nurture Mary and Jesus. He would become revered as the earthly head of the Holy Family, and he has been honored for a thousand years with a feast day on March 19 as Joseph, the Husband of Mary. And because Joseph is known for working with his hands as a carpenter, Pope Pius XII, in 1955, honored him as Joseph the Worker with a second feast day on May 1.

Might all who would hope to be "of good repute" or "gracious," and all who might be spouses, parents, workers, or members of the Catholic Church, pray for St. Joseph's intercession as we scale our own steps toward happiness, holiness, and Heaven.

Enjoying Every Excellence

Virtue directs the soul's powers to what is good; for virtue is what makes its possessors good and their activity good too.

—St. Thomas Aquinas, *Disputed Questions on Virtue*[53]

Human virtues are habits.

—St. Thomas Aquinas, *ST*, I, q. 55, art. 1

53 St. Thomas Aquinas, *Disputed Questions on Virtue*, trans. Jeffrey Hause and Claudia Eisen Murphy (Indianapolis: Hackett, 2010), 25, citing Aristotle's *Nicomachean Ethics*, 2.6.

St. Thomas's Thoughts on Philippians 4:8–9

Object of the Intellect (Truth)	Objects of the Appetite (Good)	Good beyond What Is Necessary	***Motivators of Action***	Fruits of the Acts
True	Modest (good in itself)	Lovely (leads to friendship)	***Virtue (habits within us)***	God: "The God of peace will be with you."
	Just (good directed to neighbor)	Gracious (leads to good reputation)	Praise of discipline (instruction learned from some-one else)	
	Holy (good directed to God)		Thinking (internal)	
			Doing (external)	

St. Paul	Latin Vulgate	RSVCE	St. Thomas
arete	*virtus*	excellence	virtue

Arete: The Excellence of Virtue

St. Paul goes on to tell us in Philippians 4:8 that "if there is any excellence," to think about it too. Paul used the Greek word *arete*, which is typically translated into English as "excellence," as we see in the RSVCE. Langenscheidt's *Pocket Greek Dictionary* lists possible English definitions for *arete* as follows: "goodness, excellence, perfection, merit, fitness; bravery, valor, virtue." *Virtus* is used in the Vulgate translation, from which we derive the English *virtue*, seen in English translations of St. Thomas Aquinas's Latin. Indeed, as we will soon see, in St. Thomas's extensive writings on virtue in general and a myriad of virtues in particular, he touches upon virtually every option Langenscheidt provides! But for now, let's begin at the beginning, with St. Paul's classical Greek.

The Greek word *arete* means "excellence," which, in the broadest sense, is the quality of a person or thing that does exceedingly well what it is designed to do by its nature. An excellent racehorse runs very swiftly, and an excellent draft horse can pull ponderous loads. My use of horses as one of a possible universe of examples has both a Greek and a Catholic pedigree, so to speak. In his famous moral *Encheiridion* or *Handbook*, the Stoic philosopher Epictetus writes:

> Be not elated at any excellence which is not your own. If the horse in his elation were to say, "I am beautiful," it could be endured; but when you say in your elation, "I have a beautiful horse," rest assured you are elated at something good which belongs to a horse. What, then, is your own? The use of external impressions. Therefore, when you are in harmony with nature in the use of external impressions, then be elated; for then it will be some good of your own at which you will be elated.[54]

Centuries later, the great spiritual adviser St. Francis de Sales would bring up a very similar equine theme when advising us to steer clear of the vice of vainglory:

> Vainglory is the glory that we give ourselves; either for what is not really in us, or for what is in fact in us, but not owing to anything we did, or for what is in us and owing to us but which does not deserve to be the cause of a boast.... There are those who are proud and haughty because they ride a magnificent horse or because their hat sports a fancy feather, or because they are wearing some fashionable clothing. Who does not see the folly here? If there is glory due, it belongs to the horse, the bird, or the tailor! And what a pitiable heart is his who expects esteem because of a horse, a feather, or some lace![55]

[54] *Epictetus: Discourses, Books III–IV, the Encheiridion*, trans. W. A. Oldfather (Cambridge, MA: Harvard University Press, 2000), 489.

[55] *Introduction to the Devout Life: A Popular Abridgment*, abridged by Madame Yvonne Stephan (Rockford, IL: TAN Books, 1990), 126.

Epictetus makes clear that each creature has *arete*, excellence, relative to its own nature. The excellence of a human being, however, relates not to some other creature's excellence but to an excellence that perfects our distinct nature as human beings. In Epictetus's terms, it is our ability to "use external impressions"; that is, we have been crafted in God's image as creatures with intellectual powers who can find truths and choose to act upon them. The actions of all other animals on earth are guided by instinct or training, while human actions can be guided by rational choice. Further, when we make the right choices, befitting our nature, it should bring us joy.

St. Francis de Sales elaborates on how we can fall short of the excellence possible to human beings when we strive to be honored and esteemed because of trivial things that are not truly excellent or because of excellences that are not our own. God calls every one of us to grow in the potential for excellence that He has provided us with as human beings. Jesus Christ could not have made this call any clearer: "You, therefore, must be perfect, as your heavenly Father is perfect" (Matt. 5:48).

Some biblical translations attempt to clarify St. Paul's *arete* by rendering it not merely "excellence" but "moral excellence" or "excellence of character," which is indeed the kind of excellence befitting a human being made in God's image and likeness with intellect and will. The English word *virtue* is used to mean this kind of human excellence. It derives from the Latin word *vir*, for "man," because virtues perfect us a human beings. As Aristotle wrote, "Virtue is that which makes its possessor good, and his work good likewise."[56]

[56] *Nicomachean Ethics*, bk. 2, chap. 6, as cited in *ST*, I-II, q. 56, art. 1.

St. Thomas notes that "the act of virtue is nothing else than the good use of free will" – "good use of free will" meaning willing in accordance with right reason in service of the intellect, rather than according to unregulated desires at the service of our passions. He also notes that "virtue denotes a certain perfection of a power," in particular, powers of the soul (*ST*, I-II, q. 55, art. 1). Since God has gifted human beings with many powers, there are many kinds of moral and intellectual virtues, in addition to physical kinds of excellence.

As unities of body and soul, human beings all have capacities for physical excellence that parallel the virtues of the soul. Thomas writes, for example: "Virtue, inasmuch as it is a suitable disposition of the soul, is like health and beauty, which are suitable dispositions of the body (*ST*, I-II, q. 55, art. 2). Further, "if a man uses exercise, food, and drink in moderation, he will become physically strong and his health will be improved and preserved. It is the same with the virtues of the soul—for instance, fortitude, temperance, and the other virtues.[57] Certainly, developing a virtuous soul and a vigorous body are things worth thinking about and acting upon. But how do we build virtues in our soul—or health in our bodies? Let's go to Thomas to find out.

How to Get into the Habit of Virtue

Virtues are dispositions and tendencies we work to build in ourselves so that when faced with situations requiring the use of our various powers, we will be inclined to use them rightly to achieve the good. Just as *virtue* is essentially a *good habit* that

[57] St. Thomas Aquinas, *Commentary on* Nicomachean Ethics, 89, addressing Aristotle's *Nicomachean Ethics*, bk. 1, chap. 2.

leads to good or meritorious acts, *vice* is essentially a *bad habit* that leads to evil acts of sin. How do we acquire virtuous habits as opposed to vicious ones? By working to form *good habits*, Thomas says, following Aristotle. Aristotle said we become builders by building and harpists by playing the harp. So, too, do we become virtuous people by performing virtuous acts—even if, at first, such actions do not come easy to us. It is a similar situation in the opposite direction when it comes to vice and sin. Although, unfortunately, some vicious acts are easy to do, since they flow from our selfish desires for pleasure, esteem, revenge, and so forth, when we perform vicious acts repeatedly, they become bad habits, our default responses when we are faced with moral dilemmas.

Aristotle also wrote that three things are required for virtue—namely, "to know, to will, and to work steadfastly."[58] Well, let's begin by making sure we know some important things about natural virtues.

Natural Virtues That Do Good

Natural virtues were known to Socrates, Plato, Aristotle, the Stoics, and other great pagan philosophers who were careful students of human nature. There are "moral virtues" that help us *do* the good and "intellectual virtues" that help us *know* what is truly good, as we will examine a few pages down the road. The most fundamental of the moral virtues have been known as the four *cardinal virtues*, since they "are about those things upon which a human life is chiefly occupied, just as a door turns upon a hinge"

[58] *Nicomachean Ethics*, bk. 2. chap. 4, as in *ST*, I-II, q. 55. art. 1.

(*ST*, II-II, q. 123, art. 7). (*Cardo* is Latin for "hinge.") Let's recall that all four can be seen hanging together in Scripture. For one example: "And if any one loves righteousness, her labors are virtues; for she teaches self-control and prudence, justice and courage; nothing in life is more profitable for men than these" (Wisd. 8:7).

- *Temperance* (or self-control) perfects our capacity to regulate and rein in our concupiscible appetite, which drives us toward pleasures, so that we can seek what is truly good.
- *Prudence* perfects our ability to determine the proper means to achieve the good and to act upon them.
- *Justice*, as we saw in this book's third chapter, perfects the capacity of our will to seek and do good, not only for ourselves but to render everyone his rightful due.
- *Fortitude* (or courage) perfects our capacity to harness our irascible appetite to do battle with that which raises our ire, so to speak, to do battle with or to endure difficult things that would keep us from the good.

Aristotle was famous for emphasizing an important aspect of virtue that clearly demarcates it from vice. His idea has become known as "the golden mean." "Nothing in excess" was a related Greek maxim inscribed in the forecourt of the Temple of Apollo at Delphi. It means that moral virtue lies between the vices of the extremes—between *deficiency* on one side and *excess* on the other. Note well, however, this does *not at all* imply that one should be sure not to become *too* virtuous! The mean does not imply moral mediocrity or going halfway. Aristotle (let alone St. Thomas) would not have us join the morally lukewarm who will be spit out (see Rev. 3:16)! The golden mean is no compromise between virtue and vice but is a golden peak of excellence that towers above deficiency and excess.

That golden mean, the action that is just right—not too much and not too little—will vary with the circumstances. It is up to us to exercise our powers of reasoning to find those means and, through repeated virtuous actions, to train ourselves in virtuous habits. Let's think just a bit more about the moral virtues as means of gold between vices of dross that lie on either side.

The Golden Means of the Cardinal Virtues

Vices of Deficiency	The Golden Mean	Vices of Excess
Insensibility	Temperance	Profligacy
Foolishness	Prudence	Craftiness
Personal loss	Justice	Personal gain
Cowardice	Fortitude	Rashness

Cardinal Virtues: A Parts Inventory

The four high-flying cardinal virtues do not lift our souls to their heights of excellence all by themselves. Indeed, each is aided by its own flock of affiliated virtues. In chapter 3, we examined the cardinal virtue of justice, and its flock of fellow flyers is enumerated again in a table that follows. I wonder if you recall as well that we defined three kinds of "parts" or associated virtues that accompany the cardinal virtues. To reiterate most briefly, *integral parts* are "must-haves," essential to the full operation of a cardinal virtue; *subjective parts* are specific virtues that address how the cardinal virtues are applied to specific subject matters; and *potential parts*—also called secondary or annexed virtues—per Thomas, "are the virtues connected with it, which are directed to certain secondary acts or matters, not having, as it were, the whole power of the principal virtue" (*ST*, II-II, q. 48). Let's peruse how St. Thomas laid out his parts inventory, before we think about each part a little more deeply.

The Cardinal Virtues and Their Parts

	Integral Parts	Subjective Parts	Potential Parts
Prudence	Memory	Governing self	*Eubolia*
	Reason	Governing others	*Synesis*
	Understanding	Reigning	*Gnome*
	Docility	Political	
	Shrewdness	Domestic	
	Foresight	Military	
	Circumspection		
	Caution		

	Integral Parts	Subjective Parts	Potential Parts	
Justice	Doing good	Distributive	Religion	
	Avoiding evil	Commutative	Piety	Observance
			Gratitude	Vindication
			Truth	Friendship
			Liberality	Equity
Fortitude	No separate parts; fortitude is about doing the arduous or difficult good	Magnanimity	Constancy	
		Magnificence	Confidence	
		Patience	Strenuousness	
		Perseverance	Manliness	
Temperance	Shamefacedness	Abstinence	Continence	
	Honesty	Sobriety	Mildness	
		Chastity	Meekness	
			Studiousness	
			Humility	

Prudence, often called "practical wisdom" was described by Cicero, and by Thomas's great teacher, St. Albert the Great, as consisting in three fundamental, integral parts: *memory*, *understanding*, and *foresight*; for to reach virtuous goals in the future (requiring foresight), we must take actions based upon our grasp of present situations (understanding), guided by the experiences and lessons we have learned in the past (memory). Building upon insights of the philosopher Macrobius, Thomas enumerated a full eight integral parts of prudence, adding *reason* (our ability to weigh pros and cons of potential actions rationally); *docility* (teachability), to enable us to acquire practical knowledge from others; *shrewdness* (the ability to think quickly), for situations in which we have no time to deliberate over our actions; *circumspection*, to consider all relevant circumstances; and *caution*, so that we do not rush in where angels fear to tread! (Practical suggestion: the next time you face a difficult life situation, you might want to check your inventory and see if you've brought all the integral parts of prudence into play.)

As for the subjective parts of prudence, Thomas distinguishes primarily between prudence applied to *governing ourselves* and prudence applied to *governing others*. *Reigning*, *political*, *domestic*, and *military* prudence apply to proper decision-making and execution of prudent acts needed by those who govern, those who need to obey a government, those who guide a household, and those involved in waging war or protecting the peace.

Finally, building upon the writings of Aristotle (hence the Greek words), Thomas enumerates potential or annexed virtues of *eubolia*, which means seeking good counsel from others in deciding our course of action; *synesis*, which is the virtue of making good judgments in particular matters that serve the virtue of prudence; and finally, *gnome*, referring not to a little bearded man in one's garden but to the ability to make wise, practical judgments in extreme or unusual cases. The first biblical example that comes to my mind is King Solomon's most prudent suggestion to cleave in twain the baby of disputing mothers. Now, there was gnome in action that got the job done (and, of course, saved the baby)!

Justice, I hope, has already been done justice in chapter 3, so I direct you back there if you'd care to reexamine its parts in relation to the other cardinal virtues.

Fortitude, per Thomas, has no separate integral parts because it always entails doing the arduous or difficult good.

As for its subjective parts, Thomas says there are four main parts. The first two, Thomas says, are positive parts that involve overcoming difficult obstacles. Through *magnanimity* (greatness of soul), we seek to accomplish difficult, worthwhile goals, to multiply our talents for the Master, to remove the wicker baskets from our lamps for the greater glory of God. Through *magnificence*, we strive to build great things, especially when this involves our monetary resources. Through fortitude proper, we act despite threats to our persons, and through magnificence, we act to achieve great things despite threats to our pocketbooks. The next time you consider giving to a worthwhile church or other charitable property, keep in mind that you have the opportunity to exercise the magnificent virtue of, well, magnificence. Thomas also wrote that fortitude has two enduring parts. Through *patience*, we exercise the ability to endure suffering without becoming sorrowful or defeated. It also implies an ability to endure suffering produced from the outside, from the acts of another. Indeed, if you've ever told someone, "You have the patience of a saint!" chances are that you saw that person endure with calmness and grace the less-than-neighborly behavior of another person—perhaps complaints, disrespect, or ingratitude from the very person he or she was trying to help. *Perseverance*, the second enduring virtue connected to fortitude, enables us to carry through to the end in commuting virtuous acts, regardless of how long obstacles may persist. To the magnificent man or woman, this might mean staying the course and providing whatever additional means are needed to fund a great public work beset with unexpected delays or costs. To the student, perseverance might mean continuing to study for an upcoming exam, even as the couch or the TV beckons. And in the most important sense of all, we must persevere in the faith until the end of our lives, for "he who endures to the end will be saved" (Matt. 24:13).

As for the potential parts: *confidence*, *constancy*, *strenuousness*, and *manliness*—these are allied virtues described by our great sage Cicero that enable us to act courageously in defending what's right, regardless of the magnitude or duration of obstacles we might face.

Temperance, finally, and perhaps surprisingly, consists, per St. Thomas, of integral parts of *shamefacedness* and *honesty*. Temperance reins in our passions for pleasure that, if left unchecked, would engender sins such as lust, gluttony, and drunkenness. Thomas tells us that "temperance withdraws man from things which seduce the appetite from obeying reason" (*ST*, II-II, q. 141, art. 2). Shame is what temperance flees. A temperate person will experience a shameful discomfort at the thought or reality of sinful, intemperate acts. Those lacking temperance will be shameless. (I wonder, does anyone else see how, in so many ways, our modern popular culture has lost all sense of shame, not fleeing from intemperate acts but placing them on a pedestal with a spotlight and broadcasting them throughout the world through electronic media?) As for *honesty*, Thomas elaborates that *honesty* derives from the word for "honor" (our stuff of chapter 2), and honorable things possess true excellence. The temperate person is characterized by honesty in internal thoughts, and his external acts and deeds are consistent (as we saw in the virtue of truthfulness). He or she will strive for honesty while fleeing from shame, and it will provide honor, order, and beauty to life. Indeed, Plato said that if we were to see spiritual honesty with our eyes, it would, "arouse a wondrous love of wisdom" (*ST*, II-II, q. 145, art. 2).

Subjective parts of temperance that regulate bodily desires include *abstinence*, *sobriety*, *chastity*, and *purity*. *Abstinence* is the virtue that regulates with reason our desire for and consumption of food, combatting the excess of gluttony, so that we might treat our physical bodies as temples of the Holy Spirit. *Sobriety* moderates our use of alcohol to curb excess drinking. *Chastity* takes on the challenging task of curbing our sexual longings, which are good in themselves in that they work toward the propagation of our species, but which can easily overcome our power of will and lead us on toward sin. Indeed, St. Augustine tells us that "the most difficult combats are those of chastity; whereas the fight is a daily one, but victory rare" (*ST*, II-II, q. 154, art. 3). St. Thomas also offers a tip to bolster our chastity: "Hence the most effective remedy against intemperance is not to dwell on the consideration of singulars" (*ST*, II-II, q. 142, art. 3). In other words, we should not allow our thoughts to linger on any particular person's physical body but should always remember that he or she is a soul-body unity, a child of God, a child of human parents, and perhaps now, or in the future, someone else's spouse or parent, thereby seeing that person through eyes of love instead of lust.

As for the potential or related parts of temperance, Thomas includes the virtues of *continence*, *mildness*, *meekness*, *studiousness*, and *humility*. In brief, *continence* is the virtue that enables us to use our reason to overcome inordinate desires, such as for that second donut; if practiced on a regular basis, continence may lead to full-blown temperance, by which we no longer experience an internal struggle. *Mildness* and *meekness* address how we express our anger, so that we might properly correct others and punish them if needed, but with the goal of protecting them or others and not harming the offender. We might think here of Jesus and the money changers. His actions might not seem mild and meek at first glance, until we realize that rather than chastising them and overturning their tables, He could have turned them into dust. *Studiousness* aids temperance by reining in our intellectual curiosity for things that are trivial, foolish, or harmful, so that we might focus our hearts and minds on what is truly most important—St. Paul and St. Thomas providing exquisite examples of the power of that virtue. Finally, we see that Thomas classes the foundational virtue of *humility* as an aid to temperance, since it reins in our prideful desires for things that surpass our true nature and capabilities. Indeed, Thomas notes that lowly *humility* is the perfect companion for the fortitude's ally *magnanimity*, greatness of soul, since humility reminds us that we can do nothing *on our own*, and magnanimity reminds us that, *with God*, all things are possible.

And here's something else to think about regarding the moral virtues. Every virtue that assists the four cardinal virtues has a golden mean of its own. Aristotle wrote that virtue is like hitting a target's bull's-eye, while vice and sin can miss the mark in every direction. Using *magnanimity* again as an example, a deficiency or lack of magnanimity that undershoots the mean is the vice of *pusillanimity*, which means "smallness of soul." Thomas says that this vice was displayed in the parable of the talents in Matthew 25 by the servant who buried his master's talent in the ground, rather than doing his best to make it grow. Vices on the side of excess in relation to magnanimity include *presumption*, wherein we presume our capacities are greater than they really are; *ambition*, wherein we desire not only to do great things but to dominate over others; and *vainglory*, wherein we desire not to do great things but to be praised even for trivial things or for characteristics or accomplishments that are not our own.

Natural Virtues That Seek Truth

While the natural moral virtues help us to do the *good*, the natural intellectual virtues help us to know the *true*, and hence, what is *truly good*! Ancient Greek philosophers designated three of these truth-seeking, intellectual virtues as science (or knowledge—since *scire* is Latin for "to know"), understanding, and wisdom.

You might recall as well from chapter 1 that they are right there together in Scripture as well. For example: "By wisdom a house is built, and by understanding it is established; by knowledge the rooms are filled with all precious and pleasant riches" (Prov. 24:3–5). Indeed, God Himself stands ready to give them to us if we but ask: "For the LORD gives wisdom; from his mouth come knowledge and understanding" (Prov. 2:6).

To review them again briefly:

- *Science* or *knowledge* pertains to the comprehension of cause-and-effect relationships.
- *Understanding* pertains to the grasp of fundamental, underlying principles.
- *Wisdom* pertains to the judgments made regarding the highest of causes and most fundamental of principles.

St. Thomas described their relationship like this: "Science depends on understanding as on a virtue of higher degree: and both of these depend on wisdom, as obtaining the highest place, and containing beneath itself understanding and science, by judging both the conclusions of science and of the principles on which they are based" (*ST*, I-II, q. 57, art. 2).

Recall that Thomas described virtues as perfections of the powers of our souls. So let's stop now to take a look and think about just which powers of the soul the cardinal and intellectual virtues perfect.

The Powers That Natural Virtues Perfect

Class of Virtue	Power	Virtue
Intellectual	Speculative intellect	Understanding
		Science (knowledge)
		Wisdom
	Practical intellect	Art
		Prudence
Moral	Will	Justice
	Concupiscible appetite	Temperance
	Irascible appetite	Fortitude

The intellectual virtues of the *speculative intellect* (understanding, science, and wisdom) perfect our intellectual capacities to grasp truths in a general or abstract sense as they are in themselves. The intellectual virtues of the *practical intellect* allow us to apply such knowledge in the acts of our daily lives. The virtue of *art*, as described by Aristotle, is the habit of right reason applied to making things, as we see in the artist, poet, musician, writer, craftsman, architect, and so forth. The virtue of prudence bridges the gap between intellectual and moral virtues, being in essence both, since it is the habit of right reason about getting things done in terms of the moral choices we make every day of our lives. It is closely regulated to the other cardinal moral virtues since it determines *how* we are to practice justice, temperance, and fortitude in the special acts of our lives. This is why it has been called "the charioteer of the virtues." Yet Thomas is also quick to point out that in order to think clearly enough to focus on truths, we must be able to rein in our various passions so they do not distract us and overwhelm our reason. This is where moral virtue comes to intellectual virtue's aid.

Summing Up Step 7: Excellence or Virtue

Well, I hope you'll agree that we've taken St. Paul's advice to think about whatever is excellent, since we've looked at *arete*, or *natural virtue*, from quite a few angles. And yet there are greater excellences or virtues still than any angle possible to nature. This is the realm of *supernatural virtue*, which we'll find at the last step of our ladder.

Think about This Sage #7

Aristotle

At the Olympic games the best-looking and strongest athletes do not receive the crown but the victorious competitors. So, too, among those who are good and best in virtuous living, those who perform righteous deeds become illustrious.

—Aristotle, *Nicomachean Ethics*, bk. 1, chap. 8

One way to express person's expertise in a particular subject is to exclaim, "He wrote the book on it!" Well, when it comes to *arete*, or virtue, Aristotle wrote *two* books on it, the *Eudemian Ethics* and the *Nicomachean Ethics*. Indeed, so profound is the latter book that, as I mentioned, St. Thomas Aquinas wrote a commentary on every single line of it! Let's look, for example, at a bit of elaboration Thomas provided on our quotation above:

> When he says "At the Olympic Games," he proves the same thing[59] by a custom among men. Concerning this we must know that in Macedonia there is a very high mountain called Olympus where certain competitive sports, called Olympic games, were held. In these, not the strongest and best-looking athletes but only the winning contestants received the crown, for those who did not compete were ineligible for the prize. So also, of those who are good and best in virtuous living, only those are illustrious and happy

[59] Thomas had stated in the paragraph above, "Consequently, a virtuous operation is more perfect than virtue itself." In other words, better than only to possess the capacity to act virtuously is actually to act virtuously!

> who actually perform good deeds. Hence it is better to say that happiness is a virtuous operation than virtue itself.[60]

In other words, though Aristotle was a brilliant philosopher and, indeed, "the Father of Logic," he did not meticulously study and explain the virtues merely as an intellectual exercise but so that we might exercise them in our daily lives, fulfilling our human potentials that lead to earthly happiness. Aristotle died more than three hundred years before Christ was born and did not know about the higher kind of eternal crown that St. Paul would write about: "Every athlete exercise self-control in all things. They do it to receive a perishable wreath, but we an imperishable" (1 Cor. 9:25). Further, "I press on toward the goal for the prize of the upward call of God in Jesus Christ" (Phil. 3:14). Aristotle knew and treasured natural virtue as few others before him or since, yet he did not know the supernatural virtues that are infused into our souls by God, as they had not yet been fully revealed.

Still, God graced "the Philosopher" with such a powerful intellect that it seems he suspected that "heroic" or "divine" virtues might exist:

> What is the starting point of motion in the spirit? The answer then is clear; as in the universe, so there, everything is moved by God.... And the starting point of reason is not reason but something superior to reason. What then could be superior even to knowledge and to Intellect, except God?[61]

60 *Commentary on* Nicomachean Ethics, 50.

61 Aristotle, *Eudemian Ethics*, bk. 7, chap. 14, as cited in *ST*, I-II, q. 68, art. 1.

The "thing" we will think about in our next chapter will include virtues that are infused into our souls by God and gifts that guide our actions by "something superior to reason," named "God."

Praise Be to God!

He says, "if any praise of discipline," i.e., praiseworthy knowledge, in you, do good: "teach me good judgment and knowledge" (Ps. 119:66).

—St. Thomas Aquinas, *Commentary on Philippians*

The theological virtues direct man to supernatural happiness in the same way as by the natural inclination man is directed to his connatural end.

—St. Thomas Aquinas, *ST*, II-II, q. 62, art. 3

St. Thomas's Thoughts on Philippians 4:8–9

Object of the Intellect (Truth)	Objects of the Appetite (Good)	Good beyond What Is Necessary	***Motivators of Action***	Fruits of the Acts
True	Modest (good in itself)	Lovely (leads to friendship)	Virtue (habits within us)	God: "The God of peace will be with you."
	Just (good directed to neighbor)	Gracious (leads to good reputation)	***Praise of discipline (instruction learned from some-one else)***	
	Holy (good directed to God)		Thinking (internal)	
			Doing (external)	

St. Paul	Latin Vulgate	RSVCE	St. Thomas
epainos	*laus disciplinae*	worthy of praise	praise of discipline

Instruction That Comes from God

Last in St. Paul's list of things to think about is whatever is *epainos*, usually translated into English as "praise." The RSVCE clarifies this as anything "worthy of praise." Other English translations use "praise" or "worthy of praise" most often, but synonyms such as "laudable things" and "laudable discipline" have also been used following the Latin Vulgate translation, from which the English translation of Thomas's commentary derives the phrase "praise of discipline." In the general sense of praiseworthiness, certainly every one of our prior seven things—whatever is *true, honorable, just, pure, lovely, gracious*, or *excellent*—is most praiseworthy indeed, so it seems we should think about the special sense of *epainos*, or praise, St. Paul may have had in mind. Let's turn to St. Thomas for clues.

In Thomas's analysis, he classifies our seventh thing, excellence or virtue, as a kind of "motivator of action" that derives from habits *we build in ourselves*, while he classifies "praise of discipline" as a motivator of action that *comes from instruction received from someone else*. Now, the use of the Latin word *disciplinae* (discipline) implies for Thomas that we have learned from someone else something praiseworthy that we have then internalized and used to regulate our own actions.

Now, one way we might distinguish between motivators that come from habits within us and motivators that derive from outside of us is to distinguish between natural virtues that sprout from our human nature (the intellect and moral virtues of our last chapter) and another, higher, more powerful set of virtues that are infused into our souls through the grace of God and made available to us as *disciples* of the *discipline* of Christ. This leads us to the realm of what are called "infused," "supernatural," or "theological" virtues, the kind of virtues whose existence Aristotle's reason suspected was possible but which were enumerated and made clear by holy revelation, courtesy of our own St. Paul!

The Most Praiseworthy Virtues of Them All

We call the three "heroic" or "divine" virtues Aristotle vaguely suggested *supernatural virtues*, because *supra* in Latin means "above," and these virtues are above and beyond nature, coming from God Himself. We also call these virtues *infused* because God directly infuses or pours them into our souls in Baptism. Finally, we call them *theological virtues* because they perfect us not only as *biological* beings but as *theological* beings, so to speak, directed toward the God in whose image and likeness we were made so that we might enjoy eternity with Him in Heaven.

Thomas tells us that limited, earthly happiness can be achieved by the natural virtues, but "the other is a happiness surpassing man's nature, and which man can obtain by the power of God alone, by a kind of participation in the Godhead, about which it is written (2 Pet. 1:4) that by Christ we are made 'partakers of the Divine nature' " (*ST*, I-II, q. 62, art. 1).

Now, what are these three amazing supernatural virtues? Let's go to Paul to find out: "So faith, hope, love abide, these three;

but the greatest of these is love" (1 Cor. 13:13), and to Thomas for some clarification:

- *Faith*, Thomas tells us, resides in the intellect and provides a certainty of belief in God and eternal bliss beyond what we can know through our senses and reason.
- *Hope* resides in the will, expressing our confidence that union with God is attainable.
- *Love* (also *charity* from the Latin *caritas*) perfects the will by seeking unity with God out of simple love for Him.

First, let's notice that, like the natural virtues, these supernatural virtues also perfect our powers—and precisely the highest of the uniquely human powers of intellect and will. Indeed, being supernatural, they also perfect our powers beyond the degree that is possible to our human nature unaided by God's grace. Next, let's think a little deeper about each of the three perfections God provides for us.

In Praise of Faith

Scripture tells us that "faith is the assurance of things hoped for, the conviction of things not seen" (Heb. 11:1). Thomas tells us that "in order that a man arrive at the perfect vision of heavenly happiness, he must first of all believe God as a disciple believes the master who is teaching him" (*ST*, II-II, q. 2. art. 3). Notice how this ties in with Thomas's description of "praise of discipline," as embracing instruction that comes from outside of us. Elsewhere Thomas distinguishes between the interior and exterior acts of worship prompted by the natural virtue of *religion* and the supernatural virtue of *faith* as follows:

> And yet the acts whereby God is worshipped do not reach out to God himself, as when we believe God we reach out

> to Him by believing for which reason it was stated . . . that God is the object of faith, not only because we *believe in a God*, but because we *believe God*. (*ST*, II-II, q. 81, art. 5, emphasis added)

The theological virtue of faith elevates and transforms the natural moral virtue of religion into a supernatural, intimate, and personal relationship with God, whom we believe because we know (recalling chapter 1) that God is truth itself!

In our modern time, it is also essential that we understand the relationship between natural reason and supernatural faith, since they are so often presented as opposites, in that one must choose, for example, between faith and reason or, as it is expressed more commonly now, between religion and science. St. Thomas made clear that there is only one truth, so the truths of reason and the truths of faith are never in conflict. Regarding their mutual alignment, twentieth-century Thomist Fr. Réginald Garrigou-Lagrange observed as follows: "Faith may be likened to the sun, and science or knowledge to a candle, but nothing needs prevent the sun and candle from shedding light on the same object together."[62]

The special truths revealed to us by God and believed by us through faith do not contradict reason, but they reveal truths to us that unaided reason cannot reach on its own, such as the fact that the one God revealed by reason is also a Trinity of Persons and that God the Son became incarnate as man. Fr. Garrigou-Lagrange's most famous student, known to us as Pope St. John Paul II, expressed the true relationship between faith and reason

[62] R. Garrigou-Lagrange, *The Theological Virtues*, vol. 1, *On Faith* (Saint Louis: B. Herder Books, 1965), 114.

most eloquently in his encyclical *Fides et Ratio* (*Faith and Reason*): "Faith and reason are like two wings on which the human spirit rises to the contemplation of truth; and God has placed in the human heart a desire to know the truth—in a word, to know himself—so that, by knowing and loving God, men and women may also come to the fullness of truth about themselves." The theological virtue of faith is lofty and praiseworthy indeed.

In Praise of Hope

St. Thomas tells us that while the *object* of hope is eternal bliss with God, the *subject* of hope (where it resides in our souls) is in the will. After the light of faith opens the eyes of our intellects to see and believe in the truth of God, our wills are drawn by hope to seek the goodness that comes from union with God and also to trust in God that He will help us attain eternal happiness with Him.

There is a sense in which the supernatural virtue of hope is akin to the natural moral virtues in that it can be seen as a golden mean between vices of deficiency. Per Thomas:

> Hope has no mean or extremes, as regards its principal object [i.e., eternal bliss with God], since it is impossible to trust too much in the divine assistance; yet it may have a mean and extremes, as regards those things a man trusts to obtain, insofar as he either presumes above his capability, or despairs of things of which he is capable. (*ST*, II-II, q. 17, art. 6)

Hope, then, can be seen as a golden mean between the vices of *presumption* (as a sin against the Holy Spirit wherein we presume that our salvation is assured through our own efforts—or perhaps even without our own efforts) and *despair* (an opposing sin against the Holy Spirit in which we give up hope of Heaven, rejecting God's generosity and mercy).

A hope that attains the golden mean trusts that God will give us all the spiritual assistance we need, both directly and through His instrument the Church, to join Him one day in Heaven, if we strive to cooperate with Him in gratitude and do our part as well. Such a hope is truly a laudable thing.

In Praise of Charity

Let's recall what St. Paul told us: "So faith, hope, love abide, these three; but the greatest of these is love." (1 Cor. 13:13). Let's think, too, about something else he told us: "Love never ends" (1 Cor. 13:8). Faith and hope are essential to every one of us as wayfarers on earth, climbing the staircase to Heaven, but when we finally arrive there, they will no longer be needed. We will not need faith in the *unseen* things of God when we see God, no longer through "a mirror dimly," but "face to face" in Heaven in the Beatific Vision (see 1 Cor. 13:12). Neither will we need to hope in God's help to get us to Heaven once we have entered those majestic pearly gates. Love, or charity, however, will reside forever and burn with intensity as never before in the presence of the Holy Trinity, the Blessed Mother, and all the blessed angels and saints. Yet even while we are still on earth, the theological virtue of charity is the most praiseworthy virtue of all. Indeed, who sang love's praises more beautifully than St. Paul?

> If I speak in the tongues of men and of angels, but have not love, I am a noisy gong or a clanging cymbal. And

> if I have prophetic powers, and understand all mysteries and all knowledge, and if I have all faith, so as to remove mountains, but have not love, I am nothing. If I give away all I have, and if I deliver my body to be burned, but have not love, I gain nothing. Love is patient and kind; love is not jealous or boastful; it is not arrogant or rude. Love does not insist on its own way; it is not irritable or resentful; it does not rejoice at wrong, but rejoices in the right. Love bears all things, believes all things, hopes all things, endures all things. (1 Cor. 13:1–7)

St. Thomas, as we saw in chapter 5, on loveliness and friendliness, defined charity as man's love for God, Jesus having called us to His intimate friendship. Thomas also called charity the mother of all the virtues, since "every virtue depends on it in a way" (*ST*, II-II, q. 22, art. 1). As prudence guides the moral virtues, finding practical *means* to virtuous ends, charity guides every single virtue whatever, so that it might achieve the virtuous *end* or goal of loving God with all that we are and loving our neighbor as ourselves. Per Thomas, the principal act of charity is to love (*ST*, II-II, q. 27, art. 1). The love of charity is an active love, expressed not only in *goodwill* toward our neighbor but in *benevolent deeds* as well.

Charity also transforms our love for God Himself, building upon faith and hope and "quickening" them or bringing them to life. Let's hear St. James on this one: "You believe that God is one; you do well. Even the demons believe—and shudder" (2:19). He later tells us, "For as the body apart from the spirit is dead, so faith apart from works is dead" (2:26). Thomas tells us about both "lifeless faith" and "living faith," and faith's life force is charity: "Each thing works according to its form. Now faith works through charity. Therefore, the love of charity is the form of faith" (*ST*, II-II, q. 4. art. 3). Charity is the God-infused perfection of the will that seeks to share God's love with our neighbors. Those who, like St. Paul, would live no longer as themselves but as Christ (see Gal. 2:20) do not let Jesus into their hearts and then go on their merry ways, without striving to share Christ's love with their neighbors with regard for their bodily and spiritual needs.

And as with the potential for a "lifeless faith," there can be a lifeless hope that seeks its own eternal bliss without "the first love of God" that "pertains to charity, which adheres to God for his own sake" (*ST*, II-II, q. 17, art. 8). True, living hope, then, is informed by the mature understanding and heartfelt conviction of the virtue of faith and made alive by the love of God and others, for their own sakes, that shines forth through the virtue of charity. It is through this living hope imbued with charity that we anticipate not only our own salvation, but our neighbors' as well. What a most praiseworthy example we find in St. Paul himself, who worked so hard, through the grace of God, not only for his salvation but for the salvation of the Corinthians and for ours as well (see 1 Cor. 15:10).

So how can we grow in love like St. Paul? Thomas tells us that although charity, as a theological virtue, is infused into our hearts by God, it can increase or decrease through our actions. Indeed, he tells us with moving eloquence how each act of charity increases within us the disposition or tendency to more charitable acts, "and this readiness increasing, breaks out into an act of more fervent love, and strives to advance in charity, and then this charity increases actually" (*ST*, II-II, q. 24, art. 6). Aristotle says we become builders by building and harpists by playing the harp. Thomas tells us we become fervent lovers by loving fervently! To become a more fervent lover, what simple loving act might *you* do for your neighbor or your spouse or child or friend when you next set this book aside?

Post-Graduate Learning from the Holy Spirit

God instructs us from outside (and, indeed, from inside us too) in a myriad of wondrous ways. In chapter 6, on graciousness, we briefly addressed some kinds of the graces He provides; now let us briefly think about one special gift set of graces through which we are literally instructed by the Holy Spirit. This glorious gift set falls under the category of sanctifying grace, which we also addressed in chapter 6. I'll repeat it here to refresh our memories before we get down to new business:

> *Sanctifying grace* is a gift from God that not only perfects the various *powers* of the soul, as the natural virtues do, but also permeates and transforms the very *essence* or nature of the human soul, from which the powers flow. Even the God-infused supernatural virtues of faith, hope, and charity derive from grace, their supernatural source. "For as the acquired virtues enable a man to walk in accordance with the natural light of reason, so do the infused virtues enable a man to walk as befits the light of grace" (*ST*, I-II, q. 119, art. 3). In terms of a pithy definition, sanctifying grace is grace given by God to a person to make him holy and to unite him to God as a participant in the divine nature.

As for God's special gift set of sanctifying graces, let's turn now to the prophet Isaiah, who knew that they would one day be bestowed upon our Savior in the greatest of measure and bestowed as well upon every one of us who would join with God through Baptism:

> There shall come forth a shoot from the stump of Jesse,
> and a branch shall grow out of his roots.
> And the Spirit of the LORD shall rest upon him,
> the spirit of wisdom and understanding,
> the spirit of counsel and might,
> the spirit of knowledge and the fear of the LORD.
> And his delight shall be in the fear of the LORD.
> (Isa. 11:1–3)

These seven "spirits" would become known through the teachings of the Catholic Church as the seven gifts of the Holy Spirit. "Fear of the Lord" appears twice in this passage. In the Latin Vulgate translation of St. Jerome, it appears first as *pietatis* (*piety* in English) and second as *timoris Domini* (*fear of the Lord* in English). These seven gifts are listed in the *Catechism of the Catholic Church* as "wisdom, understanding, counsel, fortitude, knowledge, piety, and fear of the Lord." Further: "They belong in their fullness to Christ, Son of David. They complete and perfect the virtues of those who receive them. They make the faithful docile in readily obeying divine inspirations" (1831).

There is so much to think about regarding these seven glorious gifts that one could certainly write a book about them.[63] Here,

[63] Come to think of it, I did so myself: Kevin Vost, *The Seven Gifts of the Holy Spirit: Every Spiritual Warrior's Guide to God's Invincible Gifts* (Manchester, NH: Sophia Institute Press, 2016). For any interested parties, I'll note that in 2022 I was invited by the Diocese of Springfield, Illinois, to make a series of brief video presentations on each of the gifts of the Holy Spirit for confirmandi, their sponsors, and their parents. The first one can

though, just to begin to give us something to think about that is particularly relevant to this chapter's theme, know that these gifts are indeed means of instruction from God. While natural and even supernatural virtues employ the powers of our human reason to regulate our thoughts, emotions, words, and deeds in service of God, these gifts of the Holy Spirit enable us to receive guidance not merely from our fallible intellect but through the divine inspiration of the infallible Holy Spirit Himself. *Virtues* have been likened to *oars* with which we row ourselves toward Heaven, while the Holy Spirit's gifts have been liked to *God's wind* behind our sails! God's breezes are infinitely more powerful than our own arms, yet we do have our small part to play. Regarding the relationship between *virtues* and the *gifts*, hear the words of St. Bonaventure, a great Franciscan saint and contemporary of St. Thomas Aquinas:

> Those who wish to have strong arms must give themselves to hard work. In a similar way, those who wish to have grace that strengthens them must give themselves to the practice of the virtues. The Apostle states: "By the grace of God I am what I am," and then adds, "I have labored harder than others."[64]

We should bear in mind as well that St. Thomas tells us that these seven gifts of the Holy Spirit flow through the theological virtues of faith, hope, and charity that we receive in Baptism and that become strengthened (made firm) in the aptly named

---

be seen here (and I happen to start with the story of St. Paul): https://www.youtube.com/watch?v=ONWHoQSQizU&t=30s.

64 St. Bonaventure, *Collations on the Seven Gifts of the Holy Spirit*, trans. Zachary Hayes, O.F.M. (St. Bonaventure, NY: Franciscan Institute, 2008), 36 (referencing 1 Cor. 15:10).

sacrament of Confirmation.[65] Let's finish with a brief description of each gift culled from the writings of our Angelic Doctor:

The Angelic Doctor's Quick Guide to the Gifts[66]

Gift of the Holy Spirit	Brief Description
Fear of the Lord	"The gift of fear has for its principal object God, Whom it avoids offending." (II-II, q. 141, art. 1)
Piety	"Piety, whereby we pay worship and duty to God as our Father, is a gift of the Holy Ghost." (II-II, q. 121, art. 1)
Knowledge	"Knowledge of human things is called knowledge," and regarding matters of faith, "to know what one ought to believe belongs to the gift of knowledge." (II-II, q. 9, art. 2)
Fortitude	"Fortitude as a virtue, perfects the mind in the endurance of all perils whatever; but it does not go so far as to give confidence of overcoming all dangers; this belongs to the fortitude that is a gift of the Holy Ghost." (II-II, q. 139, art. 1)

65 In the current Rite of Confirmation in the Catholic Church in the United States, the bishop invokes the seven gifts under the names of the spirits of "wisdom, understanding, right judgment, courage, knowledge, reverence, wonder and awe."

66 "The gifts are perfections of man, whereby he becomes amenable to the promptings of the Holy Ghost." *ST*, II-II, q. 68, art. 3.

Gift of the Holy Spirit	Brief Description
Counsel	"Human reason is unable to grasp the singular and contingent things which may occur," so our counsels are fearful and uncertain, hence, "in the search of counsel man requires to be directed by God who comprehends all things; and this is done through the gift of counsel." (II-II, q. 52, art. 1)
Understanding	"Man needs a supernatural light, in order to penetrate further still, so as to know what it cannot know by its natural light; and this supernatural light which is bestowed on man is called the gift of understanding." (II-II, q. 8, art. 1)
Wisdom	"The knowledge of Divine things is called wisdom," and regarding matters of faith, "to know them in themselves, by a kind of union with them, belongs to the gift of wisdom. (II-II, q. 9, art. 2) "Wisdom as a gift is more excellent than wisdom as an intellectual virtue, since it attains to God more intimately by a kind of union of the soul with Him, it is able to direct us not only in contemplation, but in action." (II-II, q. 45, art. 4)

Summing Up Step 8: Whatever Is Worthy of Praise

Ah! We have climbed the last stair of St. Paul's staircase to happiness, holiness, and highest of all, Heaven, and it is almost time to rest. We have looked at Paul's eight things from a variety of perspectives, and hopefully they no longer appear so daunting and unfamiliar, so "Greek" to us, as the old saying goes (or indeed, so Latin!). Let's rest just a bit on this top step, having reached the realm of the angels to reflect on the Angelic Doctor.

Think about This Saint #8

St. Thomas Aquinas (ca. 1225-1279)

Non nisi Te, Domine! (Nothing but You, Lord!)

—St. Thomas Aquinas

St. Paul gave us eight things to think about, and we are blessed to have Thomas's line-by-line commentaries on St. Paul's letters, including Philippians. His explanation of our core verses, Philippians 4:8–9, takes up less than two pages, and yet he provided us the theological scaffolding we've employed to build up St. Paul's eight-step staircase. Far more importantly, though, very few people have ever heeded St. Paul's advice and thought about these things more deeply than St. Thomas Aquinas.

Thomas's masterwork, the *Summa Theologica*, is more than three thousand pages long and comprises about 1.8 million words. The first of its three main "parts" addresses God and creation as it flows out from Him. The third part addresses Jesus Christ and His Church, the means through which we can returned to the God who made us. The second part addresses human nature, happiness, holiness, and virtue in hundreds upon hundreds of pages of illuminating analysis drawing on the vast stores of wisdom of the Holy Catholic Church, as expressed in the writings and lives of hundreds of great saints, theologians, and Church Fathers and Doctors, as they expand upon the lessons of Holy Scripture itself—including, in abundance, the wisdom we have received from the Holy Spirit's inspiration of "the Apostle," as Thomas calls him, our own St. Paul.

Like Paul, Thomas devoted his life to preaching Christ's gospel and to writing great works that have illuminated the minds and souls of Christians across the millennia. Paul, who was blessed with a vision of Jesus, spoke of dying to self and living in Christ, and his deeds matched his words. Thomas, near the end of his life, was also blessed with a vision of Jesus, who appeared upon the altar. He told Thomas that he had written well of Him and asked what He could give him in return. Thomas answered, "*Non nise Te, Domine!*" (Nothing but You, Lord!) St. Thomas Aquinas, pray for us!

Conclusion

Do These Things and Rejoice in the Lord!

What you have learned and received and heard and seen in me, do; and the God of peace will be with you.

—Philippians 4:9

But there are two kinds of good acts: one is internal, and he mentions it when he says, think on these things; "meditate on these things" (1 Tim. 4:15); the other is external; these do; "learn to do good; cease to do evil" (Isa. 1:16). The fruit is God, hence he says, and the God of peace shall be with you. As if to say, "if you do all these things, God will be with you": "live in peace, and the God of love and peace will be with you" (1 Cor. 13:11).

—St. Thomas Aquinas, *Commentary on Philippians*

St. Thomas's Thoughts on Philippians 4:8–9

Object of the Intellect (Truth)	Objects of the Appetite (Good)	Good beyond What Is Necessary	***Motivators of Action***	***Fruits of the Acts***
True	Modest (good in itself)	Lovely (leads to friendship)	Virtue (habits within us)	***God: "The God of peace will be with you."***
	Just (good directed to neighbor)	Gracious (leads to good reputation)	Praise of discipline (instruction learned from someone else)	
	Holy (good directed to God)		***Thinking (internal)***	
			Doing (external)	

What You Have Learned, Do

We have heeded St. Paul's advice and thought carefully about many things that are *true*, *honorable*, *just*, *holy*, *lovely*, *gracious*, *virtuous*, and *worthy of praise*, each thing reflecting in its own way the totality of truth, beauty, and goodness that exists in its perfection in its ultimate source and fulfillment—the Oneness of the Threeness that is God. Certainly, we have noticed the overlap and interrelationship between these various things; that *justice*, for example, is one of the many *virtues* and that God's *graces* include the most praiseworthy of the virtues—*faith*, *hope*, and *charity*, as well as *the seven gifts of the Holy Spirit*. Things *pure* and *holy* are *true* to their natures as God made them, not to mention *honorable*, *lovely*, and conducive to true *friendship*.

Did the Holy Spirit inspire St. Paul to arrange these eight things in a specific order, forming steps to Heaven, or was our good saint left to arrange them at will according to the order into which they flowed into the conscious awareness of his intellect? That I cannot say for sure for myself, but I can surely say that St. Thomas's orderly analysis has helped me think about each glorious thing, how they relate to one another, and how each advances us toward *happiness* (the reward of virtues of excellence), *holiness* (the purity of soul in which we honor and strive to imitate God's holiness), and ultimately, *Heaven*—the highest thing of all that unites us to God in the Beatific Vision.

Of course, there is a great deal more we can think about each of the eight things St. Paul enumerated for us. We will encounter them time and again as we read and reread Scripture, the *Catechism of the Catholic Church*, the *Summa Theologica*, and the cornucopia of writings of the great Communion of Saints, our brothers and sisters in Christ. If these eight things might capture our attention and inflame our hearts but a little more now, then the goal of this book has been achieved.

We must remember, however, that inspired minds and inflamed hearts do not achieve their ends unless they burst forth into loving thoughts, words, and deeds. St. Paul told us to "think about these things," but in no way did he imply the modern slang phrase to "*just* think about it!" St. James stands in full agreement, by the way: "Be doers of the word, and not hearers only, deceiving yourselves" (James 1:22). Indeed, as Paul wrote elsewhere: "And whatever you *do*, in word or deed, do everything in the name of the Lord" (Col. 3:17, emphasis added). Good St. Thomas expressed this lesson well when considering our call to *contemplation* as well as to *action*: "For even as it is better to enlighten than merely to shine, so is it better to give to others the fruits of one's contemplation than merely to contemplate" (*ST*, II-II, q. 188, art. 6). When we think about Paul's eight things *internally*, within our minds, we must strive to bring them to life in the *external* world, sharing their fruits with others. And finally, per both St. Paul and St. Thomas, we need to think about those very *fruits*.

Rejoice in the Peace of the Lord

More than one commentator on Philippians has noted that in 4:8–9 Paul has given a nod to the truth and the dignity that pagan philosophers have obtained and shared by applying their God-given reason to such true and praiseworthy things, and in that, I'm inclined to agree. St. Paul's meanings, however, immeasurably surpass those of the wisest philosophers of old since they are imbued with the fullness of the truths of faith that reason can only begin to fathom. Paul would have us think about all these things in the context of the Truth with a capital *T*, who is Jesus Christ. Jesus transforms and perfects all things, including our eight noble things so worthy of thinking about. Indeed, as Paul counseled his friends in Philippi, "Only let your manner of life be worthy of the gospel of Christ" (Phil. 1:27). All our thinking and doing is to be centered on and strengthened by Christ (cf. Phil. 4:13).

And as for the fruits of our thoughts and deeds on the eight things, Paul tells us, "The God of peace will be with you" (Phil. 4:9). Indeed, this is great reason to rejoice, as Paul himself tells us again and again and again: "Finally, my brethren, rejoice in the Lord" (Phil. 3:1) and "Rejoice in the Lord always; again I will say, Rejoice. Let all men know your forbearance. The Lord is at hand" (Phil. 4:4–5). So, should we heed St. Paul's advice, think about these things, and ask God for His grace that we might think about them more deeply and act them out more thoroughly and lovingly, God will be with us all our time on earth, and when the day comes on which we scale St. Paul's spiritual staircase for the very last time, we will rejoice as never before. God will illuminate our minds in Heaven to see Him in His essence in the Beatific Vision, a mere glimpse of which converted our own Saul, hater and persecutor of Christians, into St. Paul, one of the greatest champions of Christians and lovers of Jesus Christ.

Let's give Paul the last words:

> To our God and Father be glory for ever and ever....
>
> The grace of the Lord Jesus Christ be with your spirit. (Phil. 4:20, 23)

About the Author

Kevin Vost obtained his doctor of psychology degree in clinical psychology from Adler University in Chicago with internship and dissertation research at the Southern Illinois University School of Medicine, Alzheimer's Center, Memory and Aging Clinic.

Dr. Vost taught psychology and gerontology at Aquinas College in Nashville, the University of Illinois at Springfield, MacMurray College, and Lincoln Land Community College. He served as a Research Review Committee member for American Mensa and as an Advisory Board member for the International Association of Resistance Trainers.

He authored more than twenty Catholic books, through which he carried out the wisdom of his heavenly mentor, St. Thomas Aquinas: "Even as it is better to enlighten than merely to shine, so is it better to give to others the fruits of one's contemplation than merely to contemplate."

Sophia Institute

Sophia Institute is a nonprofit institution that seeks to nurture the spiritual, moral, and cultural life of souls and to spread the gospel of Christ in conformity with the authentic teachings of the Roman Catholic Church.

Sophia Institute Press fulfills this mission by offering translations, reprints, and new publications that afford readers a rich source of the enduring wisdom of mankind.

Sophia Institute also operates the popular online resource CatholicExchange.com. *Catholic Exchange* provides world news from a Catholic perspective as well as daily devotionals and articles that will help readers to grow in holiness and live a life consistent with the teachings of the Church.

In 2013, Sophia Institute launched Sophia Institute for Teachers to renew and rebuild Catholic culture through service to Catholic education. With the goal of nurturing the spiritual, moral, and cultural life of souls, and an abiding respect for the role and work of teachers, we strive to provide materials and programs that are at once enlightening to the mind and ennobling to the heart; faithful and complete, as well as useful and practical.

Sophia Institute gratefully recognizes the Solidarity Association for preserving and encouraging the growth of our apostolate over the course of many years. Without their generous and timely support, this book would not be in your hands.

www.SophiaInstitute.com
www.CatholicExchange.com
www.SophiaInstituteforTeachers.org